y Ullman Brothers.

PETERSON'S MAGAZINE

1872

Crafting with Lace

More Than 40 Enchanting Projects to Make

Joyce Elizabeth Cusick

A Sterling/Lark Book
Sterling Publishing Co., Inc.   New York

Photography: Evan Bracken, Light Reflections
Editor: Dawn Cusick
Art Director: Dana Irwin, Cris Colando
Production: Elaine Thompson, Dana Irwin
Illustrations: Joyce Elizabeth Cusick

Library of Congress Cataloging-in-Publication Data
Cusick, Joyce Elizabeth.
    Crafting with lace : more than 40 enchanting projects to make / by
Joyce Elizabeth Cusick.
      p.   cm.
    "A Sterling/Lark book."
    Includes bibliographical references (p.   ) and index.
    ISBN 0-8069-0443-7
    1. Lace craft.   2. Lace and lace making.   I. Title.
TT810.C87   1993
746'.04653--dc20   93-24784
                                            CIP

10 9 8 7 6 5 4 3 2 1

A Sterling/Lark Book

First paperback edition published in 1995 by
Sterling Publishing Company, Inc.
387 Park Avenue South, New York, N.Y. 10016

Produced by Altamont Press, Inc.
50 College Street, Asheville, NC 28801

© 1993 by Altamont Press

Distributed in Canada by Sterling Publishing
  ℅ Canadian Manda Group, One Atlantic Avenue, Suite 105
  Toronto, Ontario, Canada M6K 3E7
Distributed in Great Britain and Europe by Cassell PLC
  Villiers House, 41/47 Strand, London WC2N 5JE, England
Distributed in Australia by Capricorn Link (Australia) Pty Ltd.
  P.O. Box 6651, Baulkham Hills, Business Centre, NSW 2153, Australia

Every effort has been made to ensure that all the information in this book is
accurate. However, due to differing conditions, tools, and individual skills, the
publisher cannot be responsible for any injuries, losses, and other damages
which may result from the use of the information in this book.

Printed and bound in Hong Kong by Oceanic Printing

Sterling ISBN 0-8069-0443-7 Trade
               0-8069-0444-5 Paper

CONTENTS

INTRODUCTION

I have always loved lace. Collecting, making, designing, and sewing with it adds a special element of pleasure to my life, and just having it around seems to make every day a little brighter. This book represents an opportunity to share my love of lace and lace history with others through more than 40 craft projects.

Many of these projects are adaptations of historic lace crafts and are made with heirloom and French sewing techniques, while others are much simpler projects, and make use of fabric glue and glue guns.

Fine French sewing skills have been passed down in our family for many generations, and I have enjoyed explaining and illustrating these techniques for this book. My great grandmother, Elizabeth Chadwick Blundell, brought these skills, as well as a love of beautiful handmade lace and needlework, with her from England when she came to this country as a young wife and mother in the early 1880s. She came from Lancaster County, the garment and cloth making center of England at that time. Later, in this country, Elizabeth's daughters were taught fine sewing skills, as was customary for most young women of the Victorian era.

At age five I was already learning the fine hand stitches that would weave throughout the seams of my life. My mother, Florence (Toni) Elizabeth Brindle Brasier, encouraged me to sit beside her as she sewed and taught me her skills.My grandmother, Bertha Blundell Brindle, and her sister, my great Aunt Hilda Blundell Moreau, lived in homes decorated with many examples of their fine needlework. They patiently taught me to make lace and to embroider, and they also gave me some of their own work, which I use in my home today as beautiful symbols of their reassuring presence.

At age 17 I made my first tailored suit, which was admired by the manager of the local Singer sewing store when

HARPER'S BAZAR
A Repository of Fashion, Pleasure, and Instruction
Vol. XXII.—No. 4.
Copyright, 1889, by Harper & Brothers.
All rights reserved.
NEW YORK, SATURDAY, JANUARY 26, 1889.
TEN CENTS A COPY
WITH SUPPLEMENT

I went shopping for sewing machine needles. The manager offered me my first position in the adult world — selling, teaching, and keeping the store's books. A year later I began a two-year study of garment design and construction at Rhode Island School of Design, and although my degree from the University of Miami is in fine arts, sewing, fine needlework, and lace making have remained an important part of my life.

SOURCES OF LACE

The Victorians loved lace and surrounded themselves with it both inside and outside their homes. Machine-made lace that imitated the costly handmade laces was readily available to almost everyone at an affordable price. Dating from the late 19th and early 20th centuries,

Victorian homes were characteristically decorated with gingerbread millwork — scrolls and balusters of lacy woodwork.

The current owners of these beautiful examples of another time occasionally invite me into their homes to see how they have preserved and cared for them. Sometimes antique furniture enhances the gracious rooms, accompanied by treasured pieces of lace, arranged much as they would have been 100 years ago. Now, in the late 20th century, Victorian-style homes are a popular new-construction style, and historic buildings — along with the lace and fine needlework of that era — are being restored for current use.

Antique shops are a natural present-day adaptive use for Victorian buildings, and are often included in historic surveys. Visiting them as I go about my work as a historic preser-

vationist, intricate pieces of lace sometimes catch my eye, thus necessitating another addition to the lace collection. As each new treasure is added, I research the history of its origins, visiting libraries and acquiring books and publications from the 19th century.

Museums are another wonderful way to enjoy lace. Recently the Lace and Costume Museum of the city of Brussels loaned a collection of antique handmade lace and a collection of current handmade bobbin lace to the National Museum of Women in the Arts, in Washington, D.C. Visiting this show, I gazed with awe and increasing excitement at the beautiful lace gowns of fine Bruges lace worn by European royalty during the second half of the 19th century. Moving on to the gallery featuring the modern handmade bobbin lace, I felt as if I had journeyed into another time. Suspended from the ceiling were the most wonderful current examples of *Punto de Aria*, Italian for stitches in the air.

ABOUT THIS BOOK

In addition to the crafts, this book includes many of the historical and technical details that I researched when the pieces of lace and needlework given to me by family and friends became the start of a serious collection. Since the history of lace and fashion are intricately bound together, they are included in this book as historical context. Each chapter of projects opens with a history and then reviews the basic instructions needed to complete the projects. Note that the projects are identified by the lace symbols to indicate the level of difficulty, so you can practice your skills on a simple piece and then move on to more complicated projects. One lace symbol (✿) indicates a simple project; two symbols (✿✿) indicate an intermediate-level project; and three lace symbols (✿✿✿) indicate an advanced project. You'll notice that most of the sewing projects provide instructions for sewing by hand or machine.

The book begins with a history of lace making and its uses, along with visual examples of different varieties of lace. The second chapter explains and illustrates the basic techniques of French hand sewing and comparable machine techniques. The simpler projects in this chapter will build your skills and confidence, and prepare you for the more advanced projects such as the collars and shell blouses.

The third chapter features crafts made from antique laces, (defined here as lace made during the late 1800s and early 1900s, before 1940), and includes information on restoring stained and torn lace. Simple projects, such as the lace jabots, clutch handbags, and the wreaths, will make wonderful additions to your life or treasured gifts for someone special. More difficult designs, such as the Victorian collars and the emerald lace sampler, are also presented to challenge your creative spirit. Because of the large assortment of antique lace patterns made around the turn of the century, each project is a unique

opportunity to use and reuse treasures of the past.

The fourth chapter contains techniques and projects for modern synthetic laces. Matching and sewing modern all over lace instructions are an important part of this section. Some of the easier projects, such as the hats and picture frames, need little or no sewing, utilizing fabric glue to adhere the lace to a purchased item. There are several lace projects for Christmas ornaments that make fun projects for a holiday lace crafters party.

The fifth chapter features lace projects made from cutwork. This type of lace, which originated and developed from drawn thread work and embroidery during the 15th and 16th centuries, was the first method of making needle lace, and the precursor of many styles of lace developed in later centuries. This chapter begins with an historical context, and provides basic instructions for hand work and machine stitching.

The final chapter, Battenberg Lace Crafts, begins with historical details dating from the mid 1800s, when the tape or braid lace styles which preceded Battenberg first became popular with Victorian ladies. Utilizing a ready-made tape or braid combined with ancient needlepoint lace stitches to fill the spaces, Battenberg lace looks intricate and difficult to make. Although it is time consuming, it is actually fun to make. Projects using purchased Battenberg doilies are also included for a short-cut way to create crafts from this lovely lace.

ACKNOWLEDGEMENTS

Special thanks are given here to LaVaughn Hess, owner and proprietress of The Gingerbread House and Carriage House in Dunnellon, Florida. The Gingerbread House was a tri-gable house, a special historic house from the early 1900s, and the inspiration for one of the gingerbread house designs in the Modern Lace Crafts chapter. Although the original historic house was lost to fire in 1989, its spirit has been resurrected with a new structure built on the original site. LaVaughn loves lace and is always on the lookout for special pieces for my collection. Along with our interest in fine lace, a special friendship has developed.

Carole Oaks, owner of Argyle's Attic, also located in Dunnellon, is another friend who has helped in the search for additional examples of lace making and fine needlework techniques. Many other valued friends have helped in my lace searches — thank you.

My husband, Gene, who has become interested in my lace quest, has developed an eye for fine examples of the lace maker's art. Thanks to his patience and interest, many antique shops have been explored and enjoyed.

I'd also like to thank Jo Lydia Craven, of Micaville, North Carolina, for allowing me to photograph several pieces of her lace collection. Jo Lydia is known world-wide for her porcelain pottery, which she imprints with lace patterns before they are glazed and fired by her husband, Ian.

HISTORY OF LACE

Lace — an airy, decorative, openwork fabric with a distinct pattern — is made of thread that has been twisted, plaited, looped, or knotted by means of a needle, bobbin, hook, or, more recently, by machine. The word lace comes from the Latin word *laques*, meaning noose or snare. This meaning is also shared by the old French word *laz*. An English word, lace has been used to refer to decorative openwork since 1555.

The discovery of lace crafts reaches far back into ancient times. Fine linen garments worn by the ancient Egyptians, as well as the linen strips used to wrap their mummies, provided the fabric base for early examples of needlework and openwork decoration. Samples of drawn thread work and cutwork — still in recognizable condition — were discovered late in the 19th century in the ancient tombs of the people who lived along the Nile. Lace crafts may even predate the Egyptians, dating back to the people who first spun fiber into thread and then wove the thread into cloth or twisted it into a simple braid or cord. This braid (or "lace") was used by the ancients to join their garments together, and was the precursor of the bobbin and tape laces that were created several thousand years later.

Phoenician traders, who brought fine goods to the Roman Empire (including Gaul and Britain), may

also have carried samples of the early art of lace crafts to the Scandinavians. Evidence of this theory was revealed in 1767, when a fragment of aged and blackened gold lace was excavated from an ancient Scandinavian grave site in the vicinity of Wareham, in Dorsetshire, England. This ancient example of lace exhibited a very early design known as the lozenge pattern. Gold needles have also been found in early Danish burials.

During the Middle Ages, a transition period between the end of early Greek and Roman times during the fifth century and the beginning of the Renaissance in the 15th century, lace-like work was made in con-

vents all over Europe, as well as in England and Russia. Among other changes, the demise of the Roman Empire resulted in a strengthening of the Christian church in the west, with power vested in the pope and a rise in monastic orders. Monks and nuns, within the religious orders of the church, were responsible for preserving the knowledge of the ancient classical world, including the needlework and lace-making skills that would lend so much to modern day life. The Christian church also provided a unifying influence among the feudalistic people of Europe and England, who were engaged in endless disputes between leaders of the many small strongholds as well as in fighting off invasions by barbarians.

Patterns of the lace-like work produced in the Middle Ages consisted of the ancient lozenge design, the fleur-de-lis and other foliage designs, monsters, and armorial designs, as well as the more prevalent and widely used church emblems and biblical subjects. Most Western clothing styles of the Middle Ages were simple basic robes of silk or linen decorated with embroidered or lace-like borders worn over an undergarment or chemise. Linen was the most frequently used fabric for embellishment with lace work, lending its name to household items as well as personal underclothing. As a base for the gold, silver, and silk threads, but more often by themselves, linen fabrics and thread were used to create much of the fine needlework and lace that has survived the Middle Ages and early Renaissance times, and is still held in church and museum collections. By the 14th century, darned netting, twisted network, drawn thread work, cutwork, and macramé were all made to decorate personal and household linens.

When Bysantium was conquered by the Turks in 1453, the eastern Mediterranean was closed to trade from western European countries. No longer able to procure fine fabrics and other luxuries from the East, the nobility of western Europe had to rely on their own skills and abilities to develop and maintain the courtly elegance they desired. This predicament may have fueled the beginning of the Renaissance ("the awakening"), which began the creation of the wondrous laces that have since enhanced the world. In trying to regain the luxuries of the East, European explorers discovered the Americas. Among other things, the explorers sought new sources for precious gold and silver metals, some of which were made into thread for lace

to decorate the uniforms and formal clothing of men and the elaborate gowns of noble women.

The Renaissance, which began in the wealthy city of Florence, Italy, in the early 1400s, was a time of creative development which spread north through all of Europe, renewing interest in classical styles and civilizations. Artisans infused creative design into the objects they produced, even those intended for daily living. The ancient craft of making lace, preserved by the nuns, was also enhanced and enriched by the creativity of the Renaissance until it became a form of art. Most of the styles and varieties of lace that we value today originated during the 15th through 17th centuries, primarily in western Europe.

During this time period, adornment of the individual, and thus personal lace use, became a priority for the ruling classes and those who would follow their example. Lace was prized for its beauty and value. Like jewels (and sometimes as costly), lace was a treasured possession to be acquired, worn, and handed down among the family heirlooms and treasures. Lace enriched the economies and industries of the countries who produced it, and laws were passed to control its import and export, as well as the wearing of this increasingly pricey embellishment.

Tracing the origins of a particular style and pattern of early lace is difficult because there are few written records available before 1500. Patterns were copied and adapted from one civilization to another, providing a link as to the origins of early designs. One link in this chain is apparent from the ancient Cartheginian island of Malta, where a pillow lace of geometric pattern connected with pearled bars was produced by the 16th century. Malta was located on the Phoenician trade lanes between Greece and Italy in the Mediterranean Sea, and the geometric patterns of Italian Reticella and other early cutworks appear to have been inspired by the geometric Byzantine designs of early Greek lace.

While it is generally accepted that the fine art and craft of making needlepoint lace evolved from the basic buttonhole stitch of cutwork and Reticella, there are few written records to document which country first made needlepoint lace. However, since lace patterns and techniques were distributed by the Christian church among the many convents of western Europe during the Middle Ages, it is reasonable that the basic needlepoint lace technique developed around the same time in more than one country. Several countries, including Italy, Spain, and Flanders, claim to have originated the making of needlepoint lace. From the Renaissance on, Flanders was the major lace-making country in northern Europe. Parts of Flanders were at different times annexed by both France and Spain, which may contribute to the claims of both these countries to being the first to make lace. Or, as she claims, Spain may have introduced needlepoint lace making techniques to Flanders in the 15th century.

Because the Renaissance increased literacy, many more records and inventories of various artwork and possessions of important persons were kept. These records often list lace among the most valuable goods of their owners, therefore they serve as an invaluable research source. Historic documents reveal that

HANDMADE BOBBIN LACE, C. 1900

needlepoint and bobbin lace were produced in Italy during the 15th century. An inventory in 1493 of two wealthy Italian sisters, Angela and Heppolita Sforza, Viconti of Milan, recorded personal property which included "embroidery of fine network (Lavoro a Groppi), bone lace (Lavora ad Ossa), and 12 spindle points (Punti dei Dodisi Fusi)." Pattern books of the 1500s also refer to these names among the designs for lace making. In addition to geometric patterns, some of the early designs included animals, birds, and people.

Drawings and paintings, especially portraits of Christian church dignitaries and other prominent individuals, are very helpful in determining which varieties of lace were made in each country and who wore the laces. Since dates have been established for drawings and paintings of the Renaissance, these pictorial records are among the best sources for determining where and when lace was in use, as well as documenting styles of lace at a certain period of time.

Although the Renaissance began in Italy, it was 16th-century France that quickly adopted the new ideas and set the styles of courtly fashion that were followed by the rest of Europe until the present day. France was also an important lace-making country. Stiff, geometric-patterned laces with scalloped borders were made by Queens, noblewomen, and their ladies. The intricate laces were used for the collars and ruffs (fluted neck ruffles) and the sleeve and boot ruffles that decorated the ornate courtiers' costumes, who even embellished their boots and shoes with lace rosettes.

By the 16th century, the love and use of lace had expanded from royalty and the nobility to the people involved in commerce all over Europe, as well as to the peasants, whose costumes revealed the lace-making skills of the wearers. Women edged their caps and aprons with the results of their fine lace crafts. Lace was made and in great demand everywhere in the western world.

Italy, France, and England all issued Sumptuary Laws (regulations on the use of lace), which were strictly enforced in Italy but almost ignored in France and England. Designed to limit the amount of money spent on lace and its purchase outside the country issuing the laws, the Sumptuary Laws severely limited the production of gold and silver lace. They did not seem to have much effect on the wearing of laces, especially those made of linen thread. Fortunes and lands were depleted as the upper classes tried to satisfy their desire for lace. The need for some lace apparel control during this time of lace mania is clearly revealed by a 1642 inventory of the estate of Cinq Mars, which included "300 sets collars and cuffs trimmed with lace." Smuggling became a major activity to offset the edicts against lace importation, and lace was secreted in every possible way, even in coffins, to prevent it from being discovered by officials determined to keep foreign laces from entering their countries.

The Protestant Reformation, whose Puritan styles limited the wearing of lace, was directly responsible for

many of the lace workers in Flanders emigrating to England, where they reestablished their lace

EMBROIDERED NETS WITH NEEDLE RUN LACES, C. 1870

making industry. Governments of individual countries grew stronger, while the Roman Catholic church, with its powerful papacy, lost some of its dominion over the rulers of the Western world. The Puritan rule was short-lived, though, and by the later part of the 17th century, demand for lace in England was so great that the convents and noble-women could not supply enough lace, even with the help of peasants. The lace industry was established to produce enough of the precious commodity to satisfy the return to ornate styles.

European countries produced many variations of ornate needlepoint lace

toward the middle of the 17th century. Patterns exhibited flowing sculptural designs of scrollwork and flowers, outlined by a heavier thread or cordon-net. Italy's Venetian Gros Point and Spain's Point d'Espagne are examples of the sculptured needlepoint laces. Large blossoms enhanced some of the laces, which reached their most beautiful and intri-cate designs at this time. Artists of the time fre-quently painted Dutch tulips, and tulips were especially popular worked in the bobbin lace of Flanders. Figurative designs and portraits were also created in lace. France produced magnificent needlepoint laces, includ-ing Alençon, which greatly benefit-ted the French economy during the 17th century. Beautiful silks for the courtiers' costumes were also made in France to enhance extravagant lifestyles.

In the 18th century, the large floral lace patterns of the previous centu-ry were replaced with small blos-soms scattered over a net ground, resulting in lighter needlepoint laces with more detail. Venetian needlepoint laces remained some-what formal in design. Brussels' lace makers replaced the heavy, sculp-tural pattern outlines (cordonnets) with a lighter thread of low relief. Flemish and French laces were filmy and playful. The laces and styles worn during this time period reflected the French court's ever-more frivolous lifestyle.

Also during the 18th century, jabots (also known as cravats or "falling frills") replaced the "falling collars" of 17th-century male attire. Gentlemen wore flowing, curled hairstyles and wigs complemented by less lace, while the ladies wore more lace. Layers of wide, gathered flounces adorned full skirts, while filmy lace flounces at the neckline and sleeves presented a vision of the delicate 18th-century lady resplendent in filmy lace. Soft and filmy Chantilly blonde lace, characterized by solid floral patterns united by a mesh ground, gave the illusion of being heavier than needlepoint laces, and was often used for the full skirts and gathered flounces of the mid-18th century.

Linen thread was still used for much of the lace produced before 1800, however many laces of the late 18th and early 19th centuries were made with fine cotton thread, which was introduced for making lace around 1770. Scotland's looms produced much of the cotton thread as well as an early bobbin net. Weavers experimented with stocking frame machines to develop a lace-making machine, however the machines were not perfected to produce tulle and lace until the beginning of the 19th century.

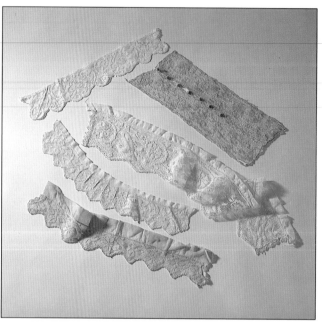

FIVE EXAMPLES OF LACE FROM THE LATE 1800s

Simple, classically styled gowns of the early 19th century were made of sheer silk and muslin (linen) fabrics complemented by light laces of patterned nets, especially Alençon, Bruxelles, and Chantilly. Bees, the symbol of Napoleon I, decorated the net ground of lace shawls with simple borders that were worn with the sheer gowns, and lace cravats tied at the throat were worn by the men. The costly, heavier needlepoint laces were relegated to the past.

By the 1820s, lace machines produced "imitation" bobbin laces, which copied or imitated the patterns and designs of "real" or hand-made bobbin lace. Further improvements to the lace machines were made in the late 1830s and early 1840s. Tapes and braids were also made on the machines. Narrow waists and full skirts returned to fashion about this time. Ball gowns worn by ladies throughout the remainder of the 19th century flaunted yards and yards of the machine-made laces. Cotton thread and mass production contributed to the less expensive laces being affordable to those who would follow the fashion.

A return to handmade lace crafts marked the mid-19th century, along with a renewed interest in the beautiful 17th-century needlepoint laces. Venetian needlepoint lace was copied for exact replicas of the precious old laces. The Venetian laces also influenced and inspired new interpretations of the scroll-work and floral patterns. Lace makers in Italy, Brussels, France, and England again produced exquisite examples of the lace makers' art, while in other countries, such as Ireland, entirely new techniques were developed. Garlands and wreaths of flowers embellished the borders of the wide lace flounces and shawls of the mid-19th century. Naturalistic floral designs incorporating roses, iris, tulips, lilies, and many other varieties of flowers and foliage flowed across full skirts made entirely of lace. Scrollwork and trellis motifs entwined the ornate blossoms of the elegant gowns worn for ceremonies and balls.

Making lace — both by machine and by hand — had become a world industry as the skills spread to the colonies of the British Empire, including India and China, along with North and South America. Women made cutwork, tape, and needlepoint laces, as well as crocheted and tatted laces for their homes and for gifts. Ladies' clothing became more tailored during the 1880s, with skirts and jackets or suits the fashionable daytime look. Chemisetts decorated with lace were worn under the jackets. By the 1890s, the Russian look became popular, with sleeves and high collars completing the lace-embellished blouses. Gracious and feminine lingerie dresses (also known as tea gowns) with lace insertions and edgings became popular, and lingerie was also embellished with lace. Men's cravats, made entirely of lace in the early 19th century, were now made from muslin or silk and were trimmed with lace or embroidery, as the fashion for wearing lace had diminished for men. Lace in men's fashions completely disappeared after the turn of the century.

Women's styles continued to be adorned with lace in the early 20th century. Although less lace

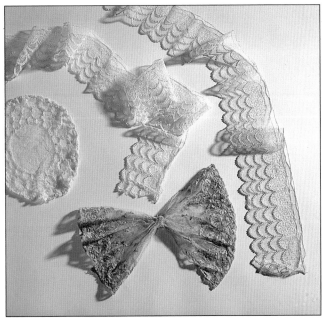

THREE EXAMPLES OF NEEDLE RUN LACE, C. 1870

appeared on the tailored dresses and suits with narrow skirts of ladies of the World War I era, lace-trimmed blouses, collars, and cuffs continued to be worn. Most of the antique lace collars and cuffs were put away for future use when the bias-cut dresses of the 1930s came into style. Evening gowns, lingerie, and children's clothes were still embellished with lace, and 20th-century bridal finery included as much or even more lace than the styles of previous centuries.

Today, antique lace machines still produce a wide variety of pattern laces made from cotton, rayon, and synthetic fibers. Lace continues to

embrace new technologies, such as the microfibers (finer than silk) that were introduced in the 1980s.

Fiber artists use the ancient techniques to create large, free-hanging pieces that are more appropriately interpreted as sculpture than embellishments for clothing. A new appreciation of real handmade lace is apparent with Museum exhibits of traditional collections of lace treasures as well as new ways of working with threads to create fantastic lace webs of pattern and design.

Much of the lace that is available today is manufactured from polyester or polyester/cotton blends. Linen thread, which is prohibitively expensive to produce in the 20th century, is seldom used for machine-made laces, although it is still in demand among those who patiently reproduce the antique patterns of fine needlepoint and bobbin laces by hand. Schools devoted to lace craft techniques have opened their doors in the lace-making countries of western Europe, as the renewed interest in lace making continues to attract those who would learn this ancient art.

ℋEIRLOOM SEWING WITH LACE

FINE FRENCH SEWING BY HAND OR MACHINE

Since ancient times, fine sewing and needlework, in addition to spinning and weaving, were the traditional skills of women. Early in the Middle Ages (fifth to 15th centuries), convents were established by the Christian church over much of Europe and England, where as early as the seventh century nuns made and adorned vestments and altar cloths.

Sewing skills were taught to the young girls of noble and well-to-do families in England and Europe, and even queens were known for their needlework. Many of these young girls were educated by the nuns from the Middle Ages on, and early collections of needlework held by the convents contain bridal gowns and laces contributed by the young women. Children of the working classes also learned to sew a fine seam and make lace.

Although dressmakers made most of their clothing, ladies and the women who attended them spent many hours of their lives with needlework in hand. Fine needlework provided an outlet for their creative needs. Needlework, tapestry, embroidery, and lace making projects recorded the important milestones of life and were often saved and passed down from one generation to another.

Because they were only worn once during each generation, christening dresses are among the heirlooms that have survived to reveal the wonderful hand sewing and lace making of early times through the 19th century.

Gathering together in their homes, women would make many of the tiny garments of the layette before the coming of a new child, an "heir." If the family was wealthy, the layette, especially the christening dress, might be commissioned from the nuns of the convents. Made of finest fabrics, these exquisite dresses were decorated with lace and embroidery by the skillful nuns, whose work brought income to their orders as well as beauty and creativity to their lives. If work is indeed a form of prayer, the Sisters of the convents were eloquent. Carefully preserved, "heirloom" christening dresses have given us a glimpse of the past, for these wonderful dresses and the lace accessories that accompany them hold an important place in the museum collections today.

Another group of garments that has always offered ladies an opportunity for using fine sewing and lace craft skills is underwear. Often we refer to underwear as "lingerie," a French word, especially if it is profusely embellished with lace, tucks, and embroidery. By the late 1800s, even when daytime styles were mostly tailored, underwear or lingerie was elaborately decorated with needlework.

The fine heirloom needlework skills of the nuns, as well as the women they taught, have been passed down to us in the form of fine "French" sewing. For while the craft of sewing began in ancient times, France was the dominant country of the

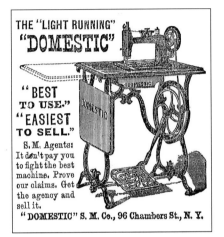

PETERSON'S MAGAZINE, 1872

Western world at the end of the Middle Ages and set the styles in fashion as well. French fashion dolls, or *Poupees,* exhibiting the latest styles, as well as French silks and laces, were sent to the courts of other European countries as gifts. *Poupees* from the court of Louis XIV, who ruled France from 1643 until 1715, were eagerly received by queens of England, Italy, and other countries. France maintained her position of fashion leadership through modern times, regardless of which country was the most powerful during succeeding centuries.

The French couture established around the middle of the 19th century brought needlework skills to their height and distributed knowledge of fine French needlework worldwide. Before the mid-19th century, it was the common practice for dressmakers to go to the wealthy, often moving into their homes and staying while whole wardrobes were completed. State gowns worn for formal court appearances were made by dressmakers or *modistes.* Tailors made the suits of the gentlemen, usually in their own shops, where the gentlemen would sometimes go for their fittings, but often the tailor, as well as the *modiste,* would bring the clothes to the wealthy or "high born" for fittings.

Charles Frederick Worth (1825–1895), an Englishman who came to Paris during the 1840s, brought about a major change in this custom. By 1857, his beautiful gowns were much in demand among the nobility. Tiring of trekking back and forth with the finery, he opened "The House of Worth" in Paris, and thereafter required anyone who wanted one of his creations to come to him. So wonderful were his fashionable gowns, made with the finest fabrics, embroideries, and laces, that the rich and powerful, as well as the

**1880'S
FRENCH SILK
DOLL'S DRESS**

colored illustrations, brought "La Mode Parisienne" into the homes of fashionable women in the United States, who often had them copied so they could wear "the latest" Paris fashions. Some of Worth's gowns were sent to America, and as an article in *Harper's Bazaar* on January 26, 1889, records, they revealed styles such as the Russian-influenced high necklines as well as the use of two or more co-ordinating fabric colors that were to become so popular in the 1890s. The elaborate gowns exhibited the machine-made "imitation lace," which closely resembled the handmade varieties of the same or similar patterns from real Alençon, Valenciennes, Mechlin, and many other handmade laces.

The development of machine-made lace early in the 19th century led to the invention of the sewing machine later in the mid-1800s. The lock-stitch machine was created in 1846 by a poor American named Elias Howe, who sold his rights to an Englishman, William Thomas. Prevented by Thomas' rights from acquiring a patent in England, Isaac Merritt Singer came to the United States to obtain a patent on his improved lock-stitch machine and began the major industry of sewing by

nobility, acquiesced to his requirement. Even the Empress Eugenie, wife of Napoleon III, had Worth design her gowns.

Charles Frederick Worth's son, Jean-Philippe Worth (1856–1926), continued his father's *maison de couture*. The fame of the House of Worth spread throughout the world, and for nearly a century (1857–1956) and through four generations, the

name was synonymous with the finest of design and sewing skills. Other French couturiers followed Worth's custom and opened their own fashion houses to make Paris with its fine sewing and design the center of the fashion world.

Periodicals and magazines like *Godey's Lady's Book* and *Petersons Magazine*, complete with hand-machine. By 1861, garment factories on both sides of the Atlantic were producing ready-to-wear garments on the steam-driven industrial sewing machines. Hem stitching was also done by machine during the second half of the 19th century. Sewing machines for tailoring and dressmaking establishments, as well as the home sewer, were also manufactured by Singer and many other companies.

Advertisements for "Domestic" and "Florence" brand home sewing machines appeared in *Peterson's* magazine as early as 1872. By the 1890s, many homes had the wonderful treadle powered sewing machines, whose users translated the fine French hand sewing techniques into machine sewing especially for seams, tucks, and applying lace to fabric. Fine French hand sewing skills remained in use for details and finishing, and even though the machines saved many hours of work, the results still had to

appear finely finished in the manner of the French couture.

Zigzag sewing machines were introduced during the early 1950s. These machines were able to accomplish automatically in just a few minutes the stitches that the home sewer had previously managed in long hours by working from side to side with the fabric placed in an embroidery hoop. Today, the standard of fine French sewing remains, whether the work is accomplished by the modern electronic versions of the early sewing machines or done by hand in the traditional manner of fine needlework.

Fabrics and Laces

The basic skills of fine French sewing included in this section have instructions for both hand and machine sewing methods. The decision to use one or the other is often influenced by the fabric and laces being used. The finer the fabric and lace, the more hand sewing might be utilized. Time is also a factor with

most of us, so using a combination of machine and hand stitches is recommended to complete the heirloom sewing projects included in this book.

Fine fabrics and laces should be used in making heirloom projects. After all, if an article is to be worn with pleasure and pride by one generation and then passed along to following generations, the

ALL THREE ILLUSTRATIONS
GODEY'S LADY'S BOOK, 1857

materials should be long-lasting. Cotton and linen fibers have long proven their durability; but more than that, fine cotton batiste and Irish handkerchief linen are a pleasure to work with and probably the most comfortable fabrics to wear. While they are expensive when compared to synthetic and cotton or linen blends, natural fiber fabrics are recommended here. Both fabrics wrinkle easily, but they are "classy wrinkles."

Cotton batiste is easiest to work with for making regular straight

stitch pin tucks. Decorative twin needle machine stitch pin tucks are a part of the design of the Victorian pillow (page 40), shell blouse (page 44), Puritan collar (page 36), and the portrait collar (page 32), which were all made of fine Irish handkerchief linen. This fabric is a joy to sew with, presses beautifully, and its sheer crispness is beautiful with cotton lace. These projects would be just as nice made from a fine cotton batiste.

Silk batiste is lovely to wear and sew with for something very special, but silk lacks the long-lasting durability of fine cotton batiste and Irish handkerchief linen. Additionally, silk batiste snags so easily that it's recommended for fine lingerie or blouses that will not be subject to frequent wearing. Silk peau-de-soie, crepe, and other firmly woven silks are better for outerwear.

For practice or for items where the article is not intended for future service as a family heirloom, a polyester/cotton batiste blend will work well. The heirloom nightgown (page 45) and heirloom baby bonnets (page 51) in this section were made of this fabric. The advantage of the batiste blend is in its wash-and-wear easy care and its availability in a wide assortment of colors.

If you choose to work with a batiste blend, keep in mind that it's more difficult to make tucks with than the natural fibers, and it lacks their sheer crispness. Pima cotton and cotton/polyester broadcloth are a good choice for children's clothes or for everyday clothing.

The many delicate patterns available in fine cotton lace edgings and insertions indicates their use for heirloom and fine French sewing regardless of the fabric selected. French Valenciennes laces, as well as English Knottingham and American Val laces made by machine are reasonably priced and are used and recommended for the projects in this section. Reproduction laces are made on the antique machines, from finer threads, in many of the traditional patterns. They are more expensive, but so lovely that they are well worth the added cost for a project intended as a future family heirloom or for a very special item to wear now.

Threads and Needles

Thread for fine French heirloom sewing is usually recommended to complement the weight of the fabric and laces selected. While #50 weight cotton or cotton/polyester thread is acceptable for regular sewing, fine French sewing on fine fabrics requires at least a #60 cotton thread. It is usually available in sewing supply shops and fabric stores. The higher the number, the finer the thread. Very fine #80 thread is available mostly through mailorder sources, and is used when attaching very fine antique lace to fabric by hand.

Real silk thread is traditionally used on fine silk fabrics, although rayon thread for machine embroidery has recently become available. Rayon thread has a silky finish and is fine for the purpose it is made for, but should not be confused with real silk thread and should not be used for hand sewing because it breaks and snags very easily. Thread for hand embroidery comes in small hanks and is available in many colors. Cotton and silk threads are traditionally used for hand embroidery.

Needles for hand sewing are available in several different styles. Sharps and Betweens are most

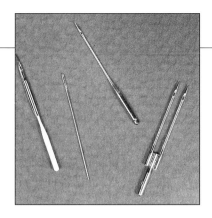

often used, with Betweens being shorter than Sharps. Embroidery needles are even longer and have larger, longer eyes to allow several strands of embroidery thread to pass through. The size of the needle should be compatible with the thread used. Number 9 or 10 Betweens seem to be best for hemming fine fabrics and attaching lace by hand. Generally, the lower the number the finer the needle (just the opposite of thread).

Machine sewing needles are available from fine sizes 8 and 9/ Metric 60, for sewing on silk and other very fine or sheer fabrics, to 10 and 11/70-80 for cotton batiste and fine linen, and 14/90 for cottons and medium-weight fabrics. Number 16/100 are used for heavier fabrics, while number 18/110 are used for heavy fabrics. Number 18s also make satisfactory holes in fine fabrics for point-de-Paris, punch work, or pin stitches. Wing-tip needles are also available for these stitches.

Twin or double needles are used for stitching regular and decora-tive pin tucks as well as machine embroidery. Other needles are available for special materials and purposes.

Revolutions in sewing machine technology have produced elec-tronic machines that can stitch many of the fine French hand sewing techniques easily and quickly, and most of the newer machines have at least a zigzag stitch. (Most of the sewing projects in this book utilize the zigzag stitch.)

Shears—scissors designed for cutting fabric—come in several lengths for the personal comfort and choice of the user. They should be kept sharp and reserved for cutting fine fabrics. (Keep another pair on hand for regular sewing needs.)

Appliqué scissors are about 6 inches (15 cm) long and enable the user to cut close to the fabric. They are used in this book for trimming fabric away from lace, trimming near seams, and for cutwork. They should not be used for cutting threads or other general purposes.

Embroidery scissors are good to keep with your hand sewing pro-jects. They average 2-1/2 to 3 inches (6 to 7 cm) long, and fit easily into a sewing kit. They are used for many of the same pur-poses as appliqué scissors as well as cutting embroidery and other threads.

All fine sewing scissors should be kept sharp and protected from non-appropriate uses. Test for sharpness by cutting a small scrap of silk fabric. If the scissors snag the silk, they should be sharpened according to their manufacturer's directions.

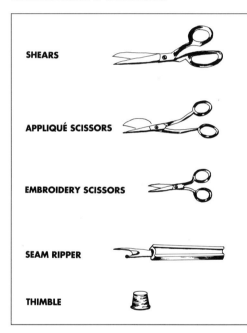

Seam rippers are also handy tools for fine sewing. Again, they should be sharp or they will snag. They should be cycled to other types of sewing the first time they snag.

Fine hand sewers use thimbles to strengthen and protect their second finger (the longest finger) from needle digs. Thimbles come in many sizes, and are also available for children. Be sure to try them on before purchasing.

For professional results, pressing is very important in fine French or heirloom sewing. The rule is: Never stitch across an unpressed seam. Projects are also easier to work on if you press after each step as indicated in the project instructions. Make sure you have a good steam iron, and choose spray sizing rather than starch because the sizing will impart a light stiffening to fine fabrics.

To press sewing projects with lace, place the project face down on a padded surface so that the pintucks, lace, embroidery, etc., will retain a raised appearance instead of being flattened into the fabric's surface. Sizing should be sprayed lightly on the back of the fabric, and then gently ironed. Set the iron's heat for the lowest heat requirement for the fiber content of your project. Always test the iron on scraps first to ensure a correct temperature setting. Allow fabric and lace to thoroughly dry before proceeding to the next sewing step.

Besides the regular padded covering on the ironing board, an additional padding is needed. About a yard (.9 m) of unbleached muslin on top of a layer of quilt batting makes the best padded surface. If you are pressing on a counter top, use two layers of quilt batting. (Have a non-flammable surface to rest the iron on as it should not be left sitting on this padded surface.)

The padded muslin can be folded and stored when not in use, and the muslin may be washed occasionally if spray sizing accumulates. Keep the muslin and quilt batting exclusively for your fine French sewing projects so you'll have a surface clear of the dyes and impurities other fabrics may impart.

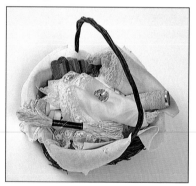

Basic Instructions

The term "Fine French Sewing" encompasses many sewing and needlework techniques, and the following instructions provide the techniques needed to complete the projects in this book. Learning these sewing skills will give you a basic introduction to fine needlework.

Fine French hand sewing begins with a 16- to 18-inch (41 to 46 cm) length of thread inserted through the needle eye. While it is possible to sew more stitches with a longer piece of thread, the longer thread tends to knot more easily and requires the hand and arm to move farther away from the work each time the needle is pulled through. To prevent the thread from pulling through, a knot is usually made at the end of the longest part of the thread. Another option is to take several stitches in one place at the beginning of the row. For rapid stitching, a short needle is desirable, and a fine #8-9-10 Between is best because it will do the least damage to a fabric. "Sharps" are a substitute and sometimes used by beginners. Several needles may be threaded and knotted before stitching commences. Use a thimble on the second or longest finger of your sewing hand to avoid the soreness that can result from using your finger to push a needle through fabric.

Running Stitch

The basic hand sewing stitch is a running stitch about 1/16 inch (1.5 mm) apart with equal spacing between stitches and a single strand of thread. Usually a number of stitches are placed on the needle before the thread is pulled through. The process is repeated until the length of the seam is completed or "run." Variations of the running stitch produce basting and gathering stitches.

Basting Stitches

Basting stitches by hand involves one short running stitch followed by a longer stitch about 3/8 to 1/2 inch (10 to 13 mm) in length. The long stitch is usually on the back side of the work so that the short running stitch pierces the fabric from back to front. This leaves the short stitch on the front as the needle again moves through the fabric to the back. Also known sometimes as tacking, basting is intended as a temporary way to hold two or more fabrics together while fitting or final sewing is under way. (*Note:* Sometimes "tacking" may also refer to several permanent stitches in one spot, where a seam isn't needed.)

Gathering Stitches

Gathering stitches are simply evenly spaced running stitches about 3/8 to 1/4-inch (10 to 6 mm) long. Two rows are usually stitched in a parallel line to add strength when they are pulled and to ensure evenly distributed gathers. Gathering stitches can be evenly distributed by pinning the end and center of the gath-

ered fabric below the line of stitches to the center and ends of the base fabric. In longer works, additional sections are pinned at one-quarter and one-eighth intervals. The threads are then firmly and gently pulled up to evenly distribute the gathers.

Machine Sewing

Fine French sewing by machine utilizes the basic lockstitch or regular sewing stitch that is found on all regular straight stitch home sewing machines manufactured since electric machines became popular in the early 1900s. The stitches are adjustable for length, and should be set for 12 to 16 stitches per inch (2-1/2 cm) on medium to fine fabrics. Unravelling is prevented by tying off the threads at the end of a seam, or by taking four or five back stitches at the beginning and end of a row. Some electronic sewing machines automatically secure the

beginning of the row and have a procedure for the end as well.

Some machines are equipped with a basting stitch, although traditionally basting has been accomplished on the home sewing machine by loosening the tension and setting the stitch length to its longest position. Gathering stitches use a setting of about eight stitches per inch, with the tension loosened on the back of the fabric. Just as with hand stitching, two parallel rows of stitches are needed. The width of the presser foot makes an excellent guide for the distance between stitching rows. Do not secure the thread at the end of the row because the thread on the back side of the fabric is pulled to distribute the gathers. (See hand sewing for instruction on evenly distributing gathers.).

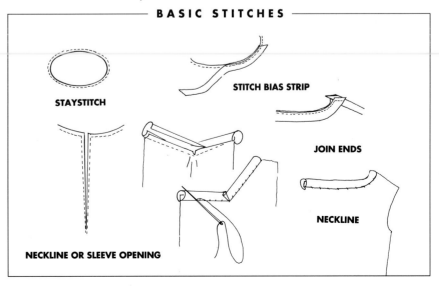

BASIC STITCHES

STAYSTITCH

STITCH BIAS STRIP

JOIN ENDS

NECKLINE

NECKLINE OR SLEEVE OPENING

French Seams

With the wrong sides of the fabric together, straight stitch (running stitch by hand) about 1/4 inch (6 mm) from the edge. Trim the fabric about 1/8 inch (3 mm) from the seam. Turn and press with right sides together.

BASIC STITCHES

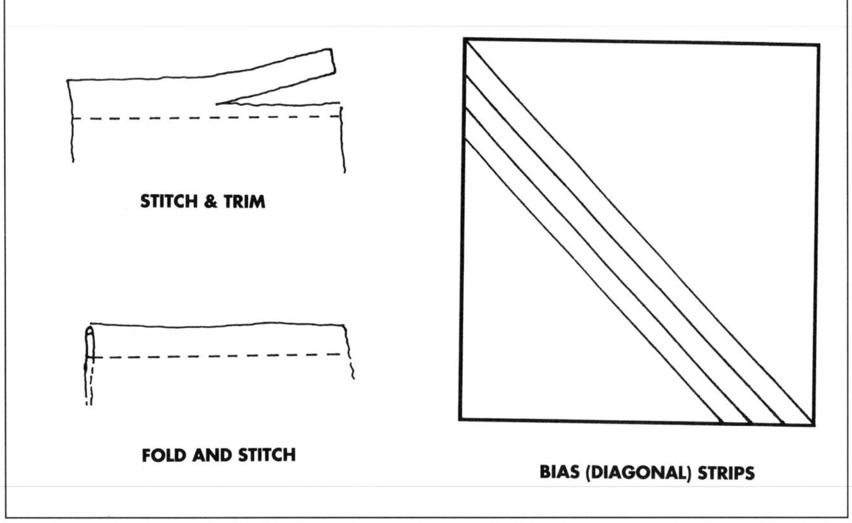

STITCH & TRIM

FOLD AND STITCH

BIAS (DIAGONAL) STRIPS

Then stitch the seam again on the wrong side of the fabric about 1/4 inch from the edge. Open to the right side and make sure that all frayed edges are contained within the seam. Press the seam on the wrong side toward the back of the garment.

French Bands or Rolled Bindings

Made from fabric cut on the true bias or diagonal of the fabric weave, French bands, also known as rolled bindings, are used to finish necklines as well as neck and sleeve openings. First cut 1-inch wide bias strips from the fabric. Then stitch around the neckline about 1/4 inch from the edge. Pin the bias strip with right sides together to the garment starting at one shoulder seam and baste. Join the ends of the bias strip at the shoulder seam by matching the edges as shown in the illustration below. Before you stitch, make sure that the finished binding will lie flat against the neckline with no tucks or puckers. Stitch on the same line as the first stitching. Trim the fabric to 1/8 inch from the seam. Fold the bias strip over to the inside of the garment, and then fold the raw edge under and blind stitch by hand. (Pick up two stitches from the edge of the rolled binding and one or two from the garment under the seam.) Hand stitching is preferable on natural fibers such as fine cotton batiste, linen, and silk fabrics. The finished binding may be 1/8 to 3/8 inches wide but should be of even width all around the neckline.

The binding may also be finished by machine stitching using the "stitch-in-the-ditch" method. After pinning and basting the folded bias strip on the inside of the neckline, stitch on the right side on the seam line. The stitches should blend in with the seam on some fine- and most medium-weight fabrics. (See illustration on page 21.) Sleeve and neck openings are also finished with the French band method; however, the stay stitching must follow the line indicated on the pattern, usually a "V" shape. The point requires extra reinforcing with three extra stitches on each side. Follow the instructions given for the neckline above, gently straightening the point while stitching the bias strip to it. This takes some practice, so try it on a scrap first.

Bias Binding with a Cord

This is a professional way to finish a neckline or sleeve where a small amount of bulk does not matter. A bias cord edge is also used at the waistline, to define seams, and to edge pillows.

Cut bias strips on the diagonal of the fabric, joining until the desired length is achieved. (See illustration.) Cut a length of cotton cord about 3 inches (7-1/2 cm) longer than the fabric. Fold the fabric to completely enclose the cord and stitch. Machine stitch close to the cord, using a cording foot if you have one. A zipper foot may be used but will not be able to stitch as close to the cord. Of course cording may also be hand stitched with a running stitch.

Baste the corded bias strip to the garment with the seam of the cording on the stay-stitched seam line of the garment, raw

BIAS BINDING WITH CORD

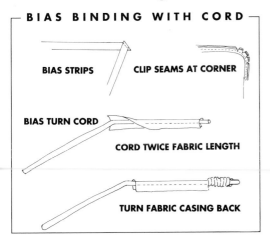

BIAS STRIPS   CLIP SEAMS AT CORNER

BIAS TURN CORD

CORD TWICE FABRIC LENGTH

TURN FABRIC CASING BACK

edges against the fabric edge. With right sides together, baste and pin the facing to the corded garment. Stitch, trim the seam allowance to about 1/4 inch (clip if the seam is on a curve), turn, and press. The cord should rise above the seam.

Bias Turn Cord

Bias turn cords are used to trim an edge such as a pillow where additional bulk of a double fabric seam is not wanted. Another use is for straps on a garment or for ribbons and bows. Allow twice as much cording as for regular bias cording. Stitch the bias strip over the cord as above, and then trim the seam to 1/4 inch and turn the fabric back on itself and the cord. The bias turn cord may also be made without the cord. Cut the strips about 1/2-inch wide and fold in half lengthwise. Then straight-stitch about 3/16-inch from the fold and turn inside out.

Pintucks

Traditional pintucks are used in a decorative manner, but they also serve to ease and gather fabric in places like the shoulder/yoke front of a dress or blouse, allowing for fullness to be released below them.

Traditional pintucks may be stitched by hand or machine with small, even, straight stitches. Mark the line of the center of each pintuck with a washable marker or basting thread. A thread may also be drawn starting at the base of the pintuck where the fullness will be released. Working on the right side of the fabric, finger press along the marked center line of the pintuck. Baste or pin about 1/16- to 1/8-inch from the edge of each tuck. Stitch by hand with a running stitch or by machine with a regular straight stitch and even tension. When all of the tucks have been stitched, tie off the threads at the base on the back/under/reverse side of the garment. Press face down on a padded surface with all of the tucks facing the front or sides going in one direction. (Tuck direction is usually determined by the design of the garment.)

ILLUSTRATIONS FROM 1904 *LADIES' HOME JOURNAL*

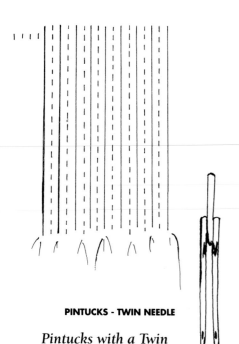

PINTUCKS - TWIN NEEDLE

Pintucks with a Twin or Double Needle

Attach the twin or double needle to your sewing machine. Adjust the stitch width to half of its maximum width or less. (The full width will break the needle.) Adjust the tension so that the double row of stitching on the front side of the fabric will be raised, while the back of the garment will lie flat and be pulled together. Attach an embroidery foot or a special pintuck foot which has ridges to guide each succeeding row of tucks. Then straight stitch along the lines marked for the pintucks. See above. Tie off the ends of the threads at the base of the tucks and press. To make decorative pintucks, use a decorative embroidery stitch. A simple

waving stitch usually works best, although you'll want to experiment with the stitches available on your sewing machine.

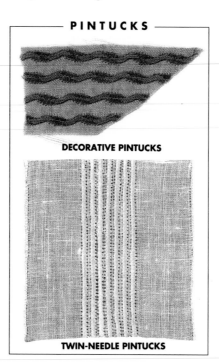

PINTUCKS

DECORATIVE PINTUCKS

TWIN-NEEDLE PINTUCKS

Hems

Hems should always be finished neatly, and there are several acceptable ways to do this. Consideration should be given to the sheerness of the fabric as well as the future use of the garment or other item. A right-handed person usually hems from right to left while a left-handed person from left to right. However, there are exceptions.

Hand-Rolled Hem

This hem is used on sheer fabrics, and the fabric should always be pressed and smooth

before beginning. Grasp the edge of the fabric at the start and roll it between your thumb and forefinger. Working on the back of the fabric, insert the needle in the hem, piercing the fabric and bringing the needle out the back and picking up one of the front threads. Repeat until the entire row is completed. The hem should roll so the stitches are not seen on the back and are almost invisible on the front. This may take some practice, so you may want to try the technique on a scrap of fabric before working on a garment.

Machine-Rolled Hem

A narrow or flange hemming attachment is used to make rolled hems on the sewing machine. Replace the regular presser foot with the hemming attachment. Stitch for 1/4 inch at the beginning of the fabric. Remove the fabric from the machine, leaving about 4 inches (10 cm) of thread to grasp. Holding the threads in your left hand, work the fabric into the hemming foot until the fabric is turning over and will slide easily. Lower the hemming foot, grasp the threads to help start the hem, and then stitch with a regular stitch. It is necessary to guide the fabric evenly into the hemmer as you stitch along the hem line. Press.

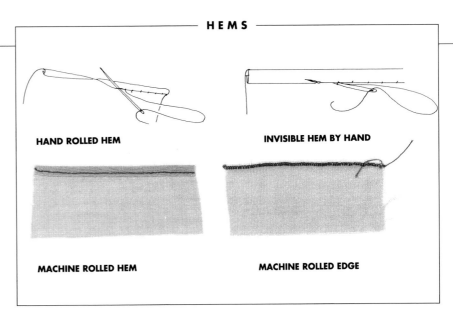

HAND ROLLED HEM

INVISIBLE HEM BY HAND

MACHINE ROLLED HEM

MACHINE ROLLED EDGE

Again, it's wise to try a practice hem or two before you work on the real thing.

Machine-Rolled Edge

Fabric edges may be finished with this technique before applying lace or in other situations where a flat finished edge is needed. First press the fabric with spray sizing and let dry. Machine stitch about 1/8 inch from the edge of the single layer of fabric. Trim close to the seam, about 1/16 inch or closer, without cutting the stitching line. Do not trim the threads at the start of the row because they help guide the fabric. Set the machine for a regular width zigzag stitch. Attach the zigzag foot with a flat bottom. (Make sure that the cover plate has the zigzag opening.) Start sewing about 1/4 inch in from the edge of the row so the fabric does not go down inside the cover plate. The left side of the zigzag stitch should cover the line of straight stitching, while the right side will be over the fabric edge. As you stitch, the fabric should roll under. Adjust the length of the stitch until it is smooth and flat. Practice first.

Invisible Hem Stitched by Hand

Measure and press the hem of your garment with the top edge folded under. Baste or tack in place. Working on the back or underside of the article, insert the needle into the folded edge of the hem, and then pull it through all the way to the knot. Working from right to left if you are right-handed (the opposite for left-handed persons), pick up one thread of the article and then two threads from the folded edge of the hem. On medium-weight fabrics, pick up two stitches of the article and two or three from the folded hem edge. Stitches should blend in with the threads of the fabric and be invisible (or nearly so) from the right side of the article. Remove basting stitches and press.

Hemstitched with Pin Stitch (Also known as Punch Stitch or Point-de-Paris Stitch)

Measure and press the hem of your garment with the top edge folded under. Baste or tack in place. Work the hem by hand on the back side of the article. Insert an embroidery or crewel needle with unknotted thread

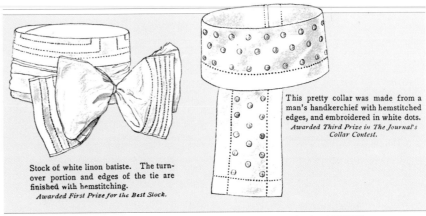

Stock of white linon batiste. The turn-over portion and edges of the tie are finished with hemstitching.
Awarded First Prize for the Best Stock.

This pretty collar was made from a man's handkerchief with hemstitched edges, and embroidered in white dots.
Awarded Third Prize in The Journal's Collar Contest.

1904 LADIES' HOME JOURNAL, SPECIAL SUMMER FASHION NUMBER

into the top edge of the folded hem, pull it through, and secure in place with three stitches at the end of the row. Insert the needle into the garment fabric at point A and back at point B, then reinsert the needle into point A and back at point C. Pull the thread tight, which should make a "pin" hole. Then insert the needle into the fold of the hem and repeat A–C along the hem line. If the fabric is of medium weight (like the linen used for hand towels), and the hem is on a straight edge, draw (pull out) one or two threads on the hem stitching line before stitching the pin stitch to create more well-defined holes. On very fine fabrics, like Irish handkerchief linen, drawing a thread usually is not necessary.

Hemstitching by Machine

Modern electronic sewing machines may have a decorative stitch for hemstitching. To use one, prepare the hem as for hand hemstitching and set the machine for a narrow width stitch. Attach a #18 or a wingtip needle, which will make the pin holes in the fabric. Practice on a scrap first as the width and length of the stitch will vary according to the fabric used. When you are satisfied with the setting, stitch along the hemline. The holes should be inserted

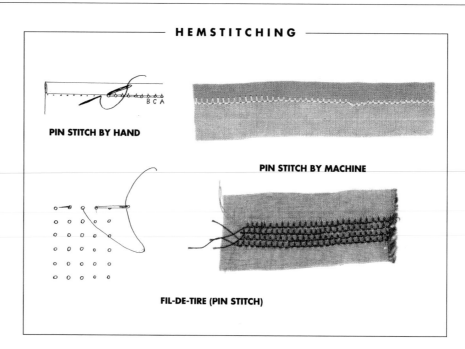

HEMSTITCHING

PIN STITCH BY HAND

PIN STITCH BY MACHINE

FIL-DE-TIRE (PIN STITCH)

into the garment while the catch stitch will penetrate all three layers of fabric. The result is a very neat and decorative finish that is quick and easy to do.

Fil-de-tire (filling) with Point-de-Paris (Also known as Pin Stitch or Punch Stitch by Hand)

A lovely, airy openwork filling may be applied to a garment pattern area with row after row of pin stitch filling. Dots about 1/8-inch apart are applied to the pattern area with a washable marking pen where each hole will be. Secure the thread on the back of the garment. Working on the right side of the fabric, insert the embroidery or crewel needle between the threads of the fabric, from the back at point A, down at point B, and

again into A, then again down at point B. This time return the needle at point C, then back down into B again, back into C, then to B again. Then work on the diagonal and return the needle at point D, then back to point A, then D, then back to A again. Continue to work the pattern in this way until the entire area is filled with evenly spaced holes. It is necessary to pull the thread taut with each stitch so that the threads of the fabric will part and form the hole.

Fil-de-tire by machine

Filling areas of pattern with pin stitch by machine is easy. First mark the dot pattern with a washable marker. Set the machine for hemstitching with the holes at the marked points. (Again practice is needed to correctly set the stitch.) With the hole on the left, stitch the first row of the pattern from the right side. Each succeeding row should be made with the right side of the machine stitch into the preceding row's pin holes. The result is taut, airy openwork that looks beautiful as well as difficult.

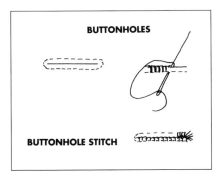

Buttonhole Stitch

The basic buttonhole stitch is one of the most versatile stitches in fine needlework. Besides finishing the raw edges of buttonholes and making button and belt loops, the buttonhole stitch is the basic stitch used for making needlepoint lace as well as cutwork, Battenberg, and other tape laces.

The basic buttonhole stitch is made by hand with a double length of thread about 32 inches (80 cm) long doubled to 16 inches (40 cm), a fine Sharp or Between needle, and at least two layers of fabric for sewing. It is worked on the right side

of the fabric. Practice on a scrap of fabric to learn the basic stitch and have a row of even stitches before attempting to make buttonholes. (*Note:* For wool or heavier fabrics, use heavier thread.)

Buttonholes

Mark the slit for the buttonhole, making it slightly longer than the button. A row of small stitches should be taken around the marked slit for the buttonhole 1/8-inch from the edge to be cut (1/16-inch for very fine fabrics or baby clothes). The reinforcing row of stitches will strengthen the completed buttonhole and provide a guide line for even stitching. Next, cut the slit.

Secure the thread on the back side of the fabric at the beginning of the row by a knot or with three small stitches taken in place. Insert the needle from back to front beneath the reinforcing stitches at the beginning of the row. Point the needle toward the slit edge and cross the thread under the needle at the edge of the opening. Pull the needle through and repeat across the row. The corners are worked with the stitches fanned out around the end, or a bar tack may be made at the end of the row. (See illustration.) Buttonholes may also be made

by sewing machine; however, instructions differ for different manufacturers. Please see your manual for information on your particular machine.

Buttonhole Loops

Loops at the edge of the fabric are often used on fine fabrics and lace. Thread the needle with a long enough thread to complete one loop. The 32-inch length is enough for small buttons. Secure the thread on the back side of the edge at A and then take a small stitch in place. Leaving enough thread to loop around the button, make the second stitch at the edge at point B, then back to A, then B, ending at point A. This results in the six strands of thread needed as a bar to work the buttonhole stitch free of the fabric. Insert the needle with the point toward

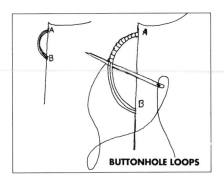

the outer edge of the loop, pass the thread under the needle (see illustration), and pull it through. Repeat the above steps for the length of the bar with all stitches facing the same way. Buttonhole loops are also used inside the edge of the fabric on the front surface of the garment to fasten hooks or at the waistline as a belt rider.

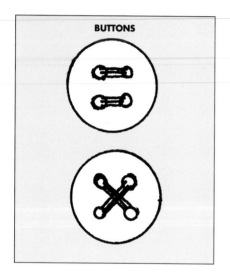

BUTTONS

Buttons

There are several ways to attach buttons with holes to fabric. The French method is tacked on the diagonal, however two parallel tacks also work. Stitching the button on top of a pin allows for some ease between the button and the fabric. When the tacks are completed, reinforce the shank area underneath the button by wrapping the thread around the stitches three or four times. Secure the thread on the back of the garment. Buttons that have smooth tops usually come with a shank that is stitched to the fabric with several tacking stitches.

Lace and Heirloom Sewing Applied with Fine French Sewing Techniques

The instructions in this section are for fine sewing with lace insertions, edgings, beading, and related decorative trimmings used to embellish the projects in the heirloom sewing and antique lace sections. Instructions for sewing with all-over lace and double galloon lace, as well as additional techniques with wide edgings and flounces, can be found in the modern lace chapter beginning on page 84.

Cotton laces are best for heirloom sewing on fine fabrics. They should be washed and pressed on a padded surface before planning and stitching begin.

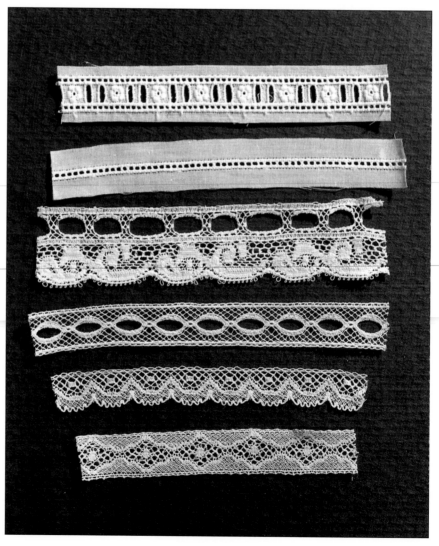

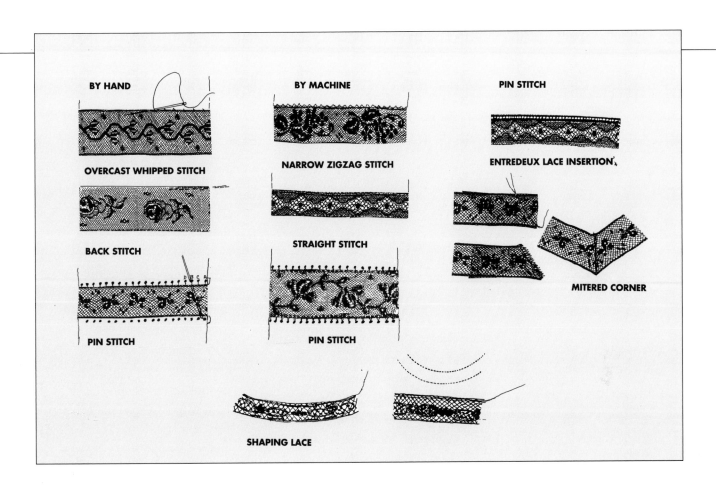

BY HAND

OVERCAST WHIPPED STITCH

BACK STITCH

PIN STITCH

BY MACHINE

NARROW ZIGZAG STITCH

STRAIGHT STITCH

PIN STITCH

PIN STITCH

ENTREDEUX LACE INSERTION

MITERED CORNER

SHAPING LACE

Lace Insertion
in Fabric by Hand

Several methods are used to insert lace into fabric by hand. Lace insertions may be placed between seams or areas of fabric. Use a fine needle and a single strand of thread 16 to 18 inches (41 to 46 cm) long unless the instructions call for something else.

The fabric edge is first turned under on the wrong side of the fabric. The lace insertion is then pinned and basted to the fabric and stitched to the fabric edge on the right side with one of the stitches described below.

1. The overcast whipped stitch is the fastest way to insert lace by hand. First insert the needle from the back of the fabric at the edge, catching the heading of the lace on the needle point as well. The next stitch whips over the edge of the insertion lace back into the fabric. Repeat the stitches about 1/16 to 1/8 inch apart.

2. The back stitch is a variation of the running stitch. First insert the needle from the back of the fabric 1/16 inch from the beginning of the row. The next stitch goes in back and comes up again 1/16 inch

in front of the first stitch, overlapping the running stitches. This stitch should produce a solid line of stitches that will blend in with the headings of the lace insertion.

3. With the pin stitch, the needle is inserted from the back of the fabric, and a thread is picked up from the lace heading. Two tiny stitches are then taken to secure the start of the row. Next, insert the needle into the right side of the fabric at point A, come up at B, go down at C, then up at point D. A thread of lace is picked up wth each stitch.

The points should be about 1/8 inch apart. Pull the thread taut with each stitch so a little hole is created. An embroidery needle may be used for this technique. (See illustration.)

Lace insertions can also be attached by machine with one of the following stitches.

1. To attach lace with a straight stitch, set the machine for a small stitch and stitch the heading of the lace to the fabric with a fine needle.

2. To attach lace with a narrow zigzag stitch, adjust the width of the stitch to about the width of the lace heading or narrower and carefully stitch along the heading of the lace.

3. To attach lace with a pin stitch, attach a #18 or wing needle to your machine. Set the machine for the hem-stitching pattern and stitch. The holes should be in the fabric while the other side of the stitch catches the lace.

Shaped Lace Insertion

Draw the outline of the design with a washable marker or pencil. Pull the larger thread in the header of the lace or stitch a gathering thread along the lace heading. Pin the ungathered edge of the lace insertion to the outside edge of your design shape. Gently pull up the gathering thread to provide ease in the other edge of the lace and pin to the inside curve of the shaped design. Baste both sides of the lace insertion to the fabric, then stitch in place with one of the techniques given above. Remove the basting threads and press face down on a padded surface with spray sizing. Allow the article to completely dry on a flat surface before handling.

The next step is to slowly, *carefully* trim away the fabric underneath the lace. Appliqué scissors, embroidery scissors (rounded points are easier to work with for beginners), or a seam ripper with the ball point inserted between the fabric and the lace are used here. Work slowly and practice on a scrap of fabric first because it is very easy to cut the lace. If machine zigzag or pin stitches have been used to stitch the lace, trim the fabric near the stitching line, taking care not to cut the stitches. If hand stitching has attached the lace, trim the fabric to 1/8 inch from the line of stitches and press back on the wrong side of the article.

Lace Edgings

Lace edgings and lace beadings may be attached to fabric in the same manner as the lace insertion directions given above or they may be stitched to entredeux, which is then stitched to the fabric or other lace. Entredeux is French for "between two," and is used to create an airy, light, open-work appearance between laces or lace and fabric. There are several methods of attaching entredeux to lace and fabric. Consideration should be given to the fabric and laces used before choosing the method. For very fine fabrics and reproduction or antique laces, overcasting or whipping the lace to the entredeux by hand is rec-ommended. Stitching on your sewing machine with a zigzag stitch works well on most other fabrics and laces and is recom-mended for children's clothes.

To whipstitch or overcast stitch by hand, trim the fabric away from one side of the entredeux. Place the right side of the lace against the right side of the entredeux. Working on the entredeux side, attach the thread to the lace side and insert the needle through the lace into the first entredeux hole. Whip or overcast from hole to hole through the lace. When the row is completed, turn the lace and entredeux right side up and finger press flat. A second piece of lace can be attached to the other side of the entredeux using the instructions given above.

To whipstitch or zigzag by machine, first trim the entredeux

ENTREDEUX/LACE

LACE/LACE

LADE EDGING

and position it on the lace as above. Set your machine for a narrow zigzag stitch with the length just long enough to place one stitch in each hole of the entredeux. On the left, stitch into the entredeux hole; on the right, stitch off the lace heading until the entire length is completed. Open and finger press as above.

Now trim the entredeux and lay it beside the lace heading with both pieces facing up. Set the sewing machine on a zigzag stitch as directed above with the needle down in the fifth hole of the entredeux. Do not try to start on the edge or the lace may be caught in the machine. Stitch from the entredeux to the lace and then back to the entredeux. This takes a little practice but is easy to do once you learn the technique.

Untrimmed entredeux may also be attached to fabric with a hand or machine straight stitch. First place the right sides together. Work on the entredeux side with a hand running stitch or by machine with a straight stitch along the edge of the entredeux. Trim the seam to about 1/8 inch from the entredeux, and finish with an overcast or zigzag stitch. Last, press the narrow seam allowance toward the fabric.

Attaching Lace to Lace

Lace may be stitched directly to a second piece of lace by overlapping the headings of the two laces and then stitching them with a back stitch by hand, a straight stitch by machine, a narrow zigzag stitch by machine (about the width of one of the lace headings), or a whip or overcast stitch by hand.

Making a Fancy Band

Several pieces of insertion may be stitched to pintucked fabric, beading and lace edgings, or any combination of these to form a fancy band that is several inches wide. First, cut pieces of the assorted trims to the same length and attach them to each other using the techniques described above. If the edging is to be ruffled, allow one and a half to twice as long a length as the other trims. When the fancy band has been stitched, press it

face down on a padded surface and allow to dry.

Matching Laces and Joining the Ends of a Fancy Band

First make sure that the fancy band is not twisted. Overlap the ends and match the pattern design of the most prominent lace, and match the headings of the other trims. If beading is part of your fancy band, overlap at least three of the openings. Baste. Straight stitch along the pattern design of the laces, and then zigzag or overcast by hand twice. Zigzag around the three openings of the beading for reinforcement. Trim the excess lace, and insert ribbon into the

FANCY BAND

beading. A regular seam that is trimmed and finished to 1/8 inch may also be used. However, the beading may pull apart if strained.

ROSE MEDALLION COLLAR ❊ ❊ ❊

*I*nspired by a Victorian locket, this portrait collar can be worn with a simple dress, a suit, or with the lace insertions shell blouse on page 44. Victorian ladies usually had several collars in their wardrobes, and they became heirlooms that were cherished long after the clothing wore out. Since this project requires advanced heirloom sewing skills, it's a good idea to make several of the more simple heirloom sewing projects before you begin this one. If desired, reproduction lace may be substituted for the cotton lace.

32

MATERIALS NEEDED

1/3 yard (.3 m) fabric, Irish handkerchief linen or fine cotton batiste

2-1/2 yards (2.3 m) lace insertion,
5/8 inch (15 mm) wide

3 yards (2.7 m) lace edging, 3/4 to
1 inch (20 to 25 mm) wide

1 yard (.9 m) lace beading

1-3/4 yards (1.6 m) entredeux

1-1/2 yards (1.4 m) narrow silk or
satin ribbon

Hand sewing needle

Spool fine cotton thread #50 or #60

Spray sizing

Washable marking pencil

PROCEDURE

1. Place the pattern on the fabric's
fold and cut out the collar. Trace
the lace insertion and embroidery
designs onto the fabric with the
washable pencil.

2. Straight stitch about 1/8 inch
(3 mm) from the edge around
the collar and follow the pencil
line for the lace insertion. Stitch
rolled neck and collar edges.
Trim the seam close to the line
of stitches; then zigzag over the
edge and trim the threads.

3. Place the collar face-down on a
flat, padded surface, and press
with spray sizing and a medium-
temperature iron. Baste a piece of
fabric underneath the roses and
bow of the medallion to reinforce
the embroidered area and create a
shadow effect.

4. Attach a wing needle to the sewing
machine and pin stitch the centers
of the roses and areas of the ribbon
as indicated by the dots on the
pattern. Attach a regular needle
to the sewing machine and zigzag
satin stitch embroidery for the
roses and bow of the medallion.
(This may also be done by hand.)
Carefully trim away the underneath
piece of the fabric outside of the
embroidered design. Press face-
down with a heat setting appropriate for the lace.

5. Gather the lace insertion, pulling
the large thread or sewing gathering
threads in the lace header. Pin the
ungathered edge of the lace to the
lower edge of the collar and around
the oval shape. Ease the fullness
and baste the gathered header of
the lace to the fabric. (The fabric
will be cut away after the insertion
has been stitched by machine.)

6. Set the sewing machine to a narrow
zigzag stitch and sew the lace to the
fabric along the header of the lace
insertions. Stitch outside the oval.
Trim away the fabric from underneath the lace, taking care not to
cut the stitches or lace.

7. With the wing needle, point-de-
Paris (pin stitch) along the insertion

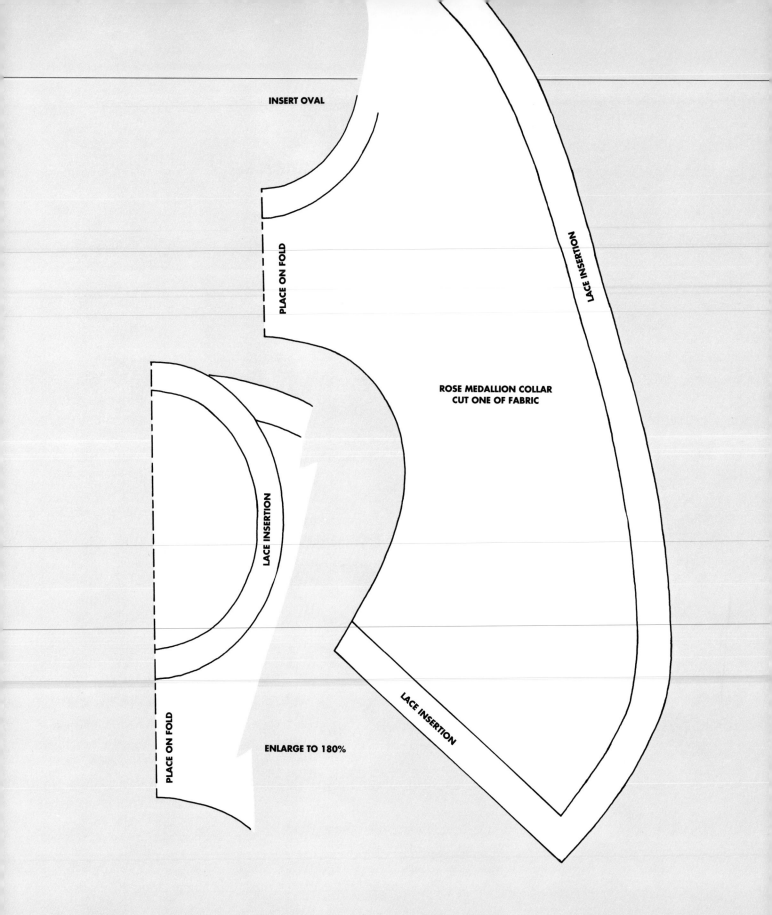

INSERT OVAL

PLACE ON FOLD

LACE INSERTION

LACE INSERTION

ROSE MEDALLION COLLAR
CUT ONE OF FABRIC

PLACE ON FOLD

LACE INSERTION

ENLARGE TO 180%

34

where it has been attached to the fabric. This can be done by hand if your sewing machine does not have the pin stitch. Place the collar face down on a padded surface. Spray it with sizing and iron with a setting appropriate for the lace.

8. Pin the lace beading to the neck's edge and stitch with a narrow zigzag to the neck's edge, extending over the collar insertion. Attach a row of insertion lace to the beading with the lace/lace method. Stitch another row of lace beading to the insertion to form the high neck.

9. Trim one side of the entredeux. Clip the other side of the entredeux at 2-inch (5 cm) intervals. Replace regular needle. Zigzag to the outer edge of the lace insertion, starting at the opening. Adjust the length of the stitch so that the needle enters each hole once. Extend the entredeux 1/2 inch below the lace edge. Attach the entredeux across the lower edge of the insertion, extending 1/2 inch at the corner. Match the holes at the corners, and trim the clipped side of the entredeux.

10. Gather the lace edging. With right sides of lace edging and insertion together, distribute the gathers evenly and baste it to the insertion so that the heading of the lace edging meets the holes of the entredeux

Attach all around the collar and top of the high neck lace band.

11. Turn the collar over so the entredeux is on top. Zigzag the lace edging to the entredeux. This step may be done by hand with a whip stitch. Gently pull the lace edging so it's flat. The entredeux holes should be open with zigzag or hand whip stitching attaching the lace.

12. Press as you did in step 7. Then thread the ribbon through the beading and tie to close at center back.

ENLARGE TO 200%

*W*orn by both men and women in the 17th century, collars were a part of everyday wear and had little or no embellishment. The style was also popular at the English court of Charles I, whose portraits reveal collars made entirely of handmade lace.

This Puritan-style collar was designed to be worn with the shell blouse on page 44.

Materials Needed

1/3 yard (.3 m) fabric, Irish handkerchief linen or fine cotton batiste

1-1/2 yards (1.4 m) lace edging, about 1/2 inch (13 mm) wide

Twin needle

Wing needle (for point-de-Paris or pin stitch)

Hand sewing needle

Fine cotton thread #50 or #60

Washable marker or pencil

Sharp scissors, appliqué scissors preferred

Spray sizing

Beauty pin or brooch for fastening (or small pearl button)

Note: 1-1/4 yards (1.1 m) reproduction or other fine cotton lace insertion, 1/2 inch wide, may be used as a pin stitch substitute.

Procedure

1. Place the pattern on the fold of the fabric. Mark the line for the pin stitch or lace insertion and cut out the collar.

2. Try on the collar. When finished with the lace edging, it should meet at the center front. Trim at the center front opening to adjust for a smaller neck or deepen for a longer neck.

3. Straight stitch about 1/8 inch (3 mm) from the edge around the collar. Stitch the rolled edge at the neckline. Trim the seam close to the line of stitches, and then zigzag over the edge and trim the threads. Press with spray sizing and a medium iron on a well-padded surface.

4. Set the sewing machine for a point-de-Paris or pin stitch and change the regular sewing needle to the wing needle. (See the detailed instructions on page 26.) Stitch three rows of pin stitch within the area indicated in the pattern.

5. Attach the twin needle to the sewing machine and stitch a decorative pin tuck or regular pin tuck about 1/4 inch (6 mm) from the pin stitch. Press again with the collar top side face-down on a padded surface. Spray with sizing and iron with a temperature setting appropriate for the lace.

6. Mark the center of the lace edging with a pin or looped thread of another color. Gather the lace edging using

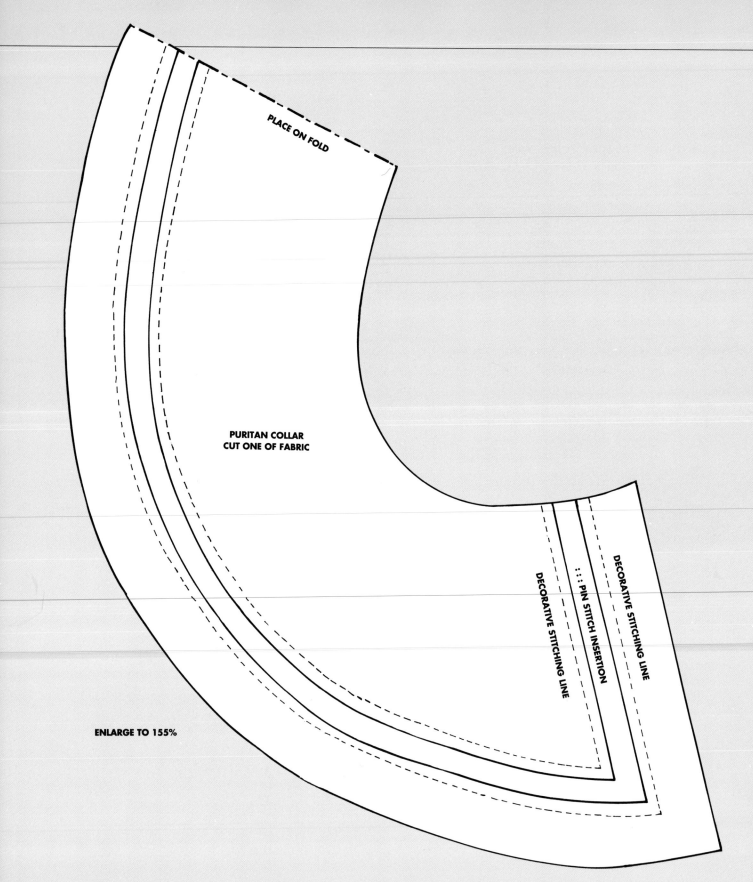

PLACE ON FOLD

PURITAN COLLAR
CUT ONE OF FABRIC

DECORATIVE STITCHING LINE

: : : PIN STITCH INSERTION

DECORATIVE STITCHING LINE

DECORATIVE STITCHING LINE

ENLARGE TO 155%

38

the heavy thread in the header, or machine stitch with a long straight stitch. Pin to the finished edge of the collar, starting at the center back and center of the lace. Ease the gathered header of the lace edging along the curved edge of the collar. Miter at the corner and continue up to the neckline opening at the top of the front. Baste.

7. Attach a wing needle. Set the sewing machine to a pin stitch (zigzag may be substituted) and slowly stitch the lace edging to the collar. Turn the neckline edge to the inside and press as directed in step 5. Fasten at the front opening with a beauty pin or brooch, or stitch a loop by hand on the right side and attach a small button on the left.

ALTERNATIVE TO PIN STITCH PROCEDURE

1. Gather the 1/2-inch lace insertion by pulling the large thread or sewing gathering threads in the lace header. Pin the ungathered lace edge to the lower edge of the insertion band or 5/8 inch (15 mm) from the edge of the collar. Ease the fullness, miter the corner, and baste the gathered header of the lace to the fabric. (The fabric will be cut away after the insertion has been machine stitched.)

2. Set the sewing machine to a narrow zigzag stitch and sew the lace to the fabric along the headers on both sides of the lace. Trim away the fabric from underneath the lace, taking care not to cut the stitches or the lace. Point-de-Paris (pin stitch) along the lace insertion where it has been attached to the fabric. This can be done by hand if your sewing machine does not have the pin stitch.

LADIES' HOME JOURNAL, 1902

VICTORIAN PILLOW

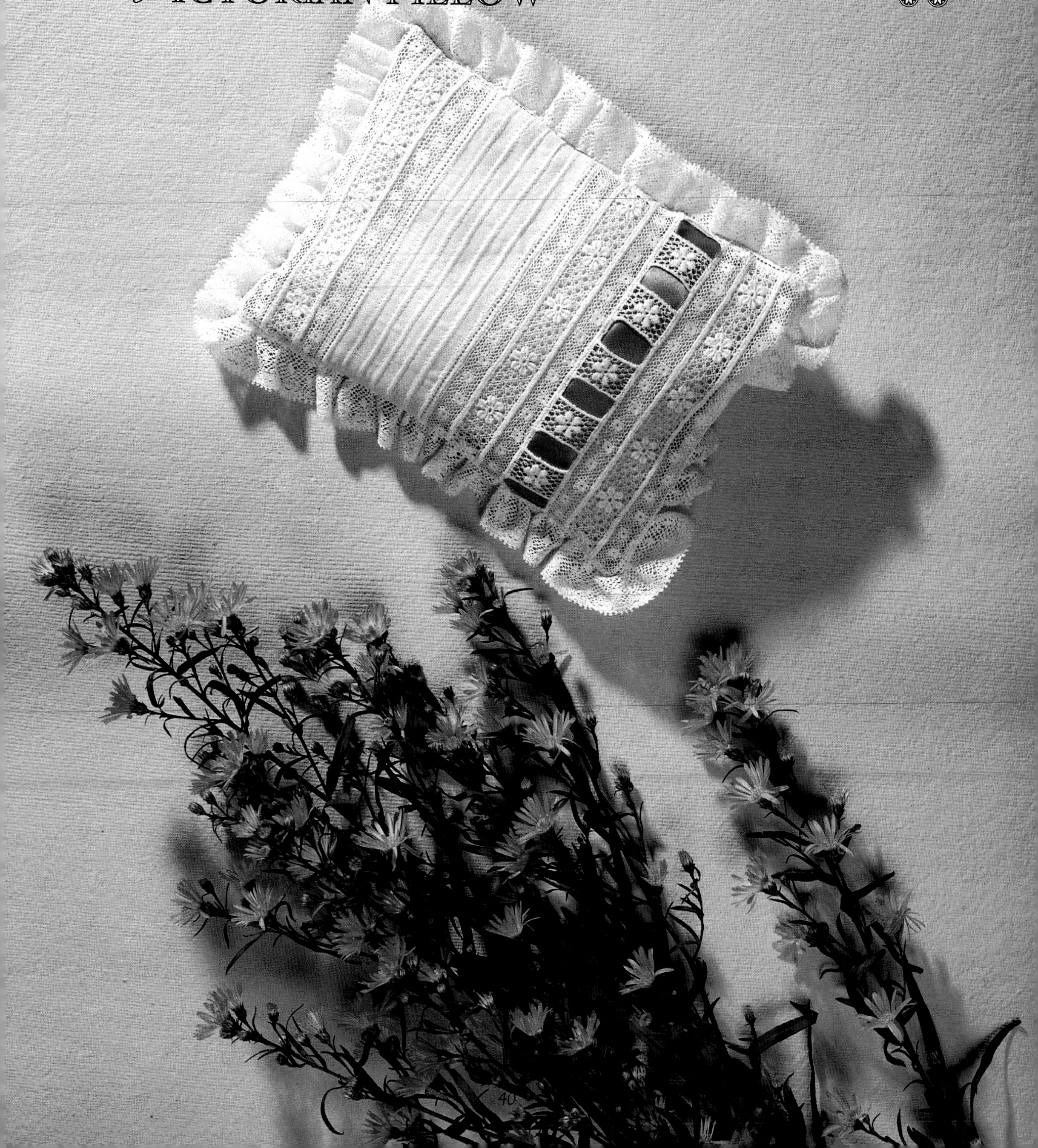

$\mathcal{V}$ictorians made small pillows from cotton batiste, silk, linen, and cotton lace. They were sometimes used to display a lady's collection of cameos and other brooches, and were passed around for everyone to admire during afternoon teas. This pillow is made with a fancy band of cotton lace in a daisy design. The materials are easily purchased in most sewing shops at a reasonable cost, making this a good project to begin learning heirloom sewing techniques.

MATERIALS NEEDED

1/4 yard (.2 m) fabric, cotton, silk batiste, or fine linen

1 yard (.9 m) small daisy cotton lace insertion, 1/2 inch (13 mm) wide

1/2 yard (.5 m) large daisy cotton lace insertion, 5/8 inches (15 mm) wide

1/4 yard cotton beading, 1 inch (2-1/2 cm) wide

1/2 yard satin ribbon in a contrasting color, 3/4 inch (20 mm) wide

1-1/2 yards (1/4 m) entredeux

1-1/2 yards cotton lace edging

Hand sewing needle

Twin needle for sewing machine

2 spools fine thread #50 or #60

Sharp scissors

PROCEDURE

1. Cut two 18-inch (46 cm) strips of the small daisy insertion and one 18-inch strip of the large daisy insertion. Set the sewing machine on the zigzag stitch with the width set to cover the headings of one edge of the lace insertion. (See illustration.) Zigzag the lace heading of one piece of small daisy insertion, overlapping the heading of the large daisy insertion by the lace/lace technique. Place the second strip of small daisy insertion on the other side of the large daisy insertion and stitch. This should result in an 18-inch strip of insertion that is the beginning of the fancy band.

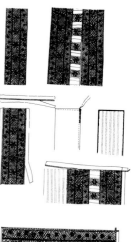

2. Cut the fancy band strip into three 6-inch (15 cm) pieces. Zigzag the piece of 1-inch-wide beading between two of the pieces to make a fancy band about 4 inches (10 cm) wide. Insert the ribbon through the beading and pin at the ends.

3. Trim one side of a 12-inch (30 cm) piece of entredeux. Cut it into 6-inch pieces and zigzag to the edge of the lace insertion of the fancy band. Set the zigzag width and length to correspond with the holes of the entredeux. Stitch into the hole, then into the lace header. Repeat step 3 with the other section of the fancy band.

4. Cut a 6-inch strip of fabric about 2-1/8 inches wide (53 mm).

Machine roll the edge by sewing along the edge with a straight stitch and then trimming close to the stitching line. Zigzag over the stitching line and off the edge of the fabric. (See illustration.)

5. Attach the twin needle to the sewing machine and thread. Stitch five rows of twin-needle pin tucks about 1/4 inch apart. Traditional pin tucks may be substituted for this step.

6. Trim the other edge of the entredeux on the fancy band strips and zigzag to the fabric. The fancy band should now measure about 8 inches (20 cm) wide. Sew across the top and bottom edge of the band with a straight stitch, and trim to even the fabric.

7. Attach the entredeux to the top and bottom edges of the fancy band with a straight stitch. Do not trim before sewing. With a narrow zigzag, stitch along the previous line of stitches to reinforce. Trim close to the stitches, but do not trim the other edge of the entredeux, since it will be used to attach the pillow back. Press face-down on a padded surface with spray sizing.

8. To make the ruffle, gather the lace edging by pulling the large thread in the lace heading. If there is none, run a row of gathering stitches along the heading. Distribute the fullness along four sides of the fancy band and pin. Baste the ruffle to the entredeux by hand, and then zigzag, catching the lace heading and holes of the entredeux. (See illustration.) Leave the edge of the entredeux for sewing to the pillow back.

9. Finish two ends of the lace edging by stitching right sides together. Trim close to the stitching line, and then sew a narrow zigzag over the stitching line. Cut two pieces measuring 6-1/2 x 5 inches (16 x 12 cm) for the pillow back, and make a hem at the center edges. Sew snaps or button and buttonhole at the center of the hem.

10. Sew the pillow back to the edge of the entredeux with a straight stitch. Be sure the right sides are together and the lace edging is safely tucked inside. Narrow zigzag and trim. Turn by unfastening the snap or button and then turning inside out.

11. Cut two pieces of fabric measuring 6-1/2 x 8-1/2 inches (16 x 21 cm) and stitch around the edge with 1/4-inch seams. Leave a 3-inch (7 cm) opening and turn. Stuff with cotton or dried herbs. (Lavender was a favorite of the Victorians.) Insert the stuffed pillow into the fancy band pillow at the back opening. *Note:* Other laces may be substituted for the fancy band. Your imagination and materials are the only limits to your creations.

INSIDE PILLOW

CUT 2

5"

6-1/2"

8-1/2"

PILLOW BACK

CUT 2

6-1/2"

HEIRLOOM SHELL BLOUSE

During the 19th century, Victorian women began wearing tailored jackets — which they did not remove in public — with their long skirts. The August, 1857, issue of "Godey's Lady's Book" shows that instead of a full blouse underneath their jackets, a "chemisette" (similar to a dickey but tied around the waist) was worn. Made of fine cotton or linen, the chemisette allowed for frequent changes and a new look each day. They were decorated with lace, pin tucks, and sometimes embroidery.

A small traveling bag containing several chemisettes and collars with cuffs could be carried aboard a train or coach to be worn during the journey, while the trunks holding the rest of her wardrobe remained undisturbed. Although dressmakers often fashioned the suits, the chemisette gave Victorian ladies an opportunity to show off their needlework skills.

Heirloom sewing experience is needed for this project, so you may want to review the instructions beginning on page 14. Reproduction or other fine cotton lace may be substituted for the pin stitch used in this project.

MATERIALS NEEDED

Shell blouse pattern

Quantity of fabric called for in pattern, Irish handkerchief linen or fine cotton batiste

Twin needle

Wing needle (for point-de-Paris or pin stitch)

Hand sewing needle

Fine cotton thread #50 or #60

Spray sizing

PROCEDURE

1. Prewash and press the fabric and lace to prevent shrinkage. Place the pattern on the fold of the fabric on the straight of the grain. Pull a thread at the center front to mark the line for pin stitch or lace insertion, and cut out the blouse. Cut a bias strip 1-1/4 inch (31 mm) wide to finish the neckline. Determine the strip's length by measuring around the pattern's neckline and adding 2 inches (5 cm).

2. Stay stitch 1/4 inch (6 mm) from the neckline's edge to prevent stretching. Place the blouse face down on a well-padded surface and press with spray sizing and a medium-temperature iron.

CONTINUED ON PAGE 48

HEIRLOOM SHELL BLOUSE ❀ ❀

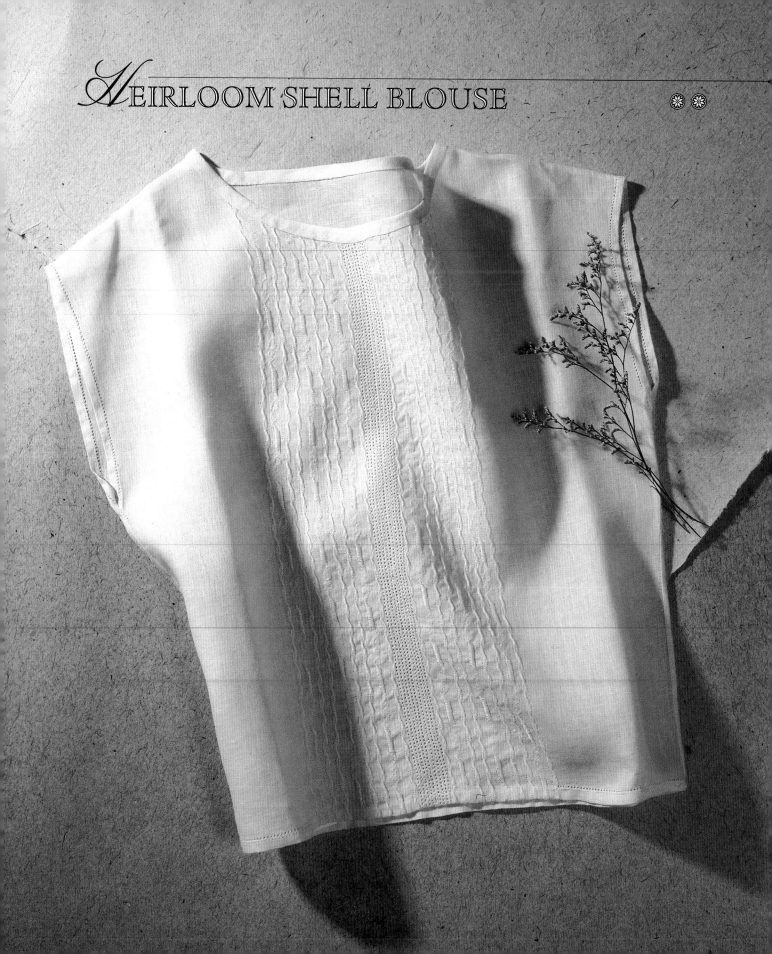

HEIRLOOM NIGHTGOWN

*L*ace has embellished ladies' underwear since the 1500s. Even when fashion dictated severe or unadorned outer clothing, lace was still a part of the delicate linens worn underneath. Lacy lingerie of soft cotton batiste, silk, or linen fabrics with cotton or silk lace makes a lovely gift or a delicate addition to your own wardrobe.

This nightgown is made with a fancy band of cotton lace and is a good project to practice your sewing skills and just enjoy the pleasures of heirloom sewing. Choose imperial batiste (an inexpensive cotton/polyester batiste) for everyday wear, or a fine cotton or silk batiste for a special-occasion gown or gift. There are many lace designs to choose from: American,

English, and French cotton laces are especially lovely with cotton batiste. Reproduction laces made from fine thread on antique lace machines would be especially lovely with silk batiste, but they're also special with fine cotton.

als in the front panel. Lengthen or shorten the length of the fabric according to the height of the individual. Be sure to purchase additional yardages of lace for larger sizes. For a child, use a fancy band 2 inches (5 cm) wide.

MATERIALS NEEDED

2 yards (1.8 m) cotton or silk batiste, 45 inches (115 cm) wide

1-1/2 yards (1.4 m) cotton lace insertion, 5/8 inch (15 mm) wide

4-1/2 yards (4.1 m) cotton lace insertion, 3/4 inch (20 mm) wide

3 yards (2.7 m) cotton lace edging

1-1/4 yards (1.1 m) entredeux

4 yards (3.6 m) satin ribbon, 1/4 inch (6 mm) wide

Hand sewing needle

Spool fine thread #50 or #60 same color as fabric

Spool fine thread #50 or #60 same color as lace

Sharp scissors

Note: The directions are given for medium (misses 10-12) size. The gown is waltz length, below the knee (42 inches, 105 cm, long) with a 3-inch (7 cm) fancy band. For larger sizes, add 6 inches (15 cm) to the bustline measurement for the length of the fancy band and add additional materi-

PROCEDURE

1. Prewash and press all materials to prevent shrinkage. Cut two 42-inch strips of wide lace insertion, one 42-inch strip of narrow insertion, and one 42-inch strip each of the lace beading, edging, and entredeux.

2. Set the sewing machine on the zigzag stitch with the width set to cover the heading of one edge of the lace insertion. (See basic instructions.) Zigzag the lace heading of one piece of the wide lace insertion to the narrow lace insertion. Stitch the second piece of wide insertion on the other side of the narrow insertion. Then stitch the lace beading to one side of the insertion strip and the lace edging to the beading strip. This should result in a fancy band of laces that's 3 inches wide. Trim one edge of the entredeux and zigzag it to the lower wide insertion edge of the fancy band.

3. Cut two 24-inch (60 cm) strips of the lace beading and the edging. Zigzag the lace heading to the beading heading for the shoulder straps. Cut two 36-inch (90 cm) strips

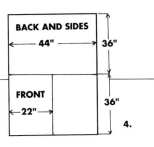

of wide lace insertion for the front fabric panel and set it aside.

4. The fabric panels will be attached to this entredeux strip. Cut two panels of fabric 36 inches long. The back and side panels will be the full 44-inch width of the fabric. For the front panel, cut the fabric 22 inches (55 cm) wide.

5. Trim the selvages from the sides of the fabric panels and finish the edges with the rolled edge technique. (See basic instructions.) Zigzag the lace insertion to the sides of the front fabric panel, and connect the back panel to the other sides of the lace insertion.

6. Join the fancy band by overlapping the ends. Straight stitch them first and then zigzag, following the lace pattern if it is distinct. Double lap the heading for a stronger seam, and trim carefully.

7. Cut the ribbon into two 34-inch (86 cm) pieces for the shoulder straps and one 60-inch (150 cm) piece for the fancy band. Insert the ribbon through both shoulder beading strips and tack at the ends. Any excess ribbon should be pulled up to form a bow that will allow for adjustment of the strap length. Insert the 60-inch ribbon strip through the fancy band, starting at the center front. The ribbon should be able to gather freely so the gown will fit comfortably.

8. Pin the shoulder straps in place on the fancy band's back 4 inches to the side of the center front and 4 inches from the center back with the lace edging on the outside. Attach the straps by zigzagging on the top of the fancy band along both headings of the lace beading.

THIS is the new lingerie waist with long, tucked sleeves and a shallow yoke of lace to match the trimming.

SUMMER FRILLS; LADIES' HOME JOURNAL, 1909.

9. Gather the top edge of the fabric panels and pin them to the fabric-edged entredeux of the fancy band. Line up the lace insertion strips of the front fabric panel with the shoulder straps. Machine stitch with right sides together, then trim the seam and zigzag to finish. Hem the lower edge of the gown with a narrow machine or hand hem. Press with a medium-temperature steam iron. (Test the iron first on scraps of fabric, lace, and ribbon.)

3. Set the sewing machine for a point-de-Paris or pin stitch and change the regular sewing needle to a wing needle. (See the detailed instructions on page 26.) Stitch nine rows of pin stitch down the center front, using the line established by the pulled thread as a guide. (Practice first on a strip of fabric.) See below for lace insertion alternative.

4. Attach the twin needle to the sewing machine and stitch a decorative or regular pin tuck on each side of the pin stitch or insertion. Leave about 1 inch of space on each side. Sew two more rows of pin tucks, then leave another 1-inch space; then sew two more rows of pin tucks, then another 1-inch space, and finish with a final row of pin tucks. (See illustration.)

5. Attach the regular needle to the sewing machine and stitch a row of embroidery stitches in each space between the pin tucks. If your machine does not have decorative machine stitches, rows of narrow lace insertion or hand embroidery can be substituted, or you can make all the rows pin tucks. Place the front of the blouse face down on a well-padded surface. Spray with sizing and press with an iron set at a temperature appropriate for the lace.

6. Try on the blouse to fit and adjust the neckline's opening. Stitch the shoulder seams with a French seam. (See basic instructions on page 22.) Press

with the seam facing toward the back.

7. Finish the neckline with a French band by attaching a bias strip of fabric to the neckline with the ends at one shoulder seam. Baste in place. Machine stitch the closing at one shoulder seam. (See basic instructions.) Press the seam and then machine stitch the band to the blouse's neckline. Remove the basting stitches and trim the seam to within 1/4 inch from the stitches. Fold the fabric evenly over the edge of the neckline, maintaining the same width all around. Press. Fold the raw edge for a finished hem, and baste in place around the inside of the neckline. The fabric should lie smoothly. Stitch by hand using the whip stitch, or by machine using the stitch-in-the-ditch method.

8. Stitch the side seams with French seams. Finish the hems at the sleeves 1/4 inch wide, and the lower edge 3/8 inch (10 mm) wide by hand; or baste them in place and then pin stitch with a wing needle by machine.

ALTERNATIVE TO PIN STITCH INSERTION

Begin with 2/3 yards (.6 m) lace insertion, 1 to 2 inches (2-1/2 to 5 cm) wide, and 3 yards (2.7 m) narrow insertion. Baste the lace insertion at the center front. Set the sewing machine's zigzag stitch to a narrow width and sew the lace to the fabric along the headers of both sides of the lace insertion. Trim away the fabric from underneath the lace, taking care not to cut the stitches or lace.

*L*ACE SACHETS

1 piece cotton lace edging, 6 inches long

1/2 yard (.5 m) narrow satin ribbon

Hand sewing needle

1 spool fine thread #50 or #60

Note: Lace widths may be substituted as long as the overall 4- x 6-inch (10 x 15 cm) dimension remains the same.)

*F*illed with lavender, rose petals, and other fragrant herbs, the Victorians used sachets to fragrance their linens and lingerie. Little girls would often make them for gifts as they were learning the fine needlework skills that were an important part of their daily lives. Today, these sachets make good practice projects for learning heirloom sewing stitches and are also a fun way to experiment with mixing different laces and embroideries together.

MATERIALS NEEDED

2 pieces narrow cotton lace insertion, 6 inches (15 cm) long

2 pieces cotton lace insertion, 6 inches long and 3/4 inch (20 mm) wide

1 piece cotton embroidered or lace beading, 6 inches long

2 pieces entredeux, 6 inches long (not needed if the beading is edged with it)

PROCEDURE

1. Cut two 6-inch strips from each lace insertion. Set the sewing machine on the zigzag stitch with the width set to cover the headings of one edge of the lace insertion. Zigzag the lace heading of one piece of narrow insertion, overlapping the heading of the second wider lace insertion by using the lace/lace technique.

2. Place the second strip of narrow insertion on the other side of the wide insertion and stitch. Next, attach the second strip of wide insertion. This should result in a strip of insertion measuring 2-3/4 x 6 inches (6 x 15 cm) that is the beginning of the fancy band.

3. If your beading does not have an entredeux edge, trim one side of a 12-inch (30 cm) piece of entredeux. Cut it into two 6-inch pieces, and zigzag it to both edges of the lace beading. Set the zigzag width and

LACE SACHETS

length to correspond with the holes in the entredeux. Stitch into a hole, then into the lace header. Repeat to the end of the row.

4. Zigzag the piece of beading to the lace fancy band, which should now be about 3-1/4 inches (7 cm) wide. Zigzag the lace edging to the other side of the beading. Press with spray sizing face-down on a padded surface.

5. Fold with right sides together so the sachet is a double thickness about 3 inches wide and 4 inches high (7-1/2 x 10 cm). Stitch a 1/8 inch (3 mm) seam along the edge of the side and bottom. Turn right sides out. Insert the ribbon through the beading and make knots at each end. Stuff with fragrant dried herbs or flowers. Pull the ribbon tight and tie into a bow. If desired, the outside of the sachet can be decorated with dried or silk flowers hot-glued to the bow.

ℬABY BONNETS ✦ ✦

𝒜 small bonnet of cotton batiste, silk, or linen fabrics with cotton or silk lace makes a wonderful gift for a new baby. If the new baby has an older sister, you may want to make an extra bonnet for big sister's favorite baby doll. This bonnet is made with a fancy band of cotton lace using a puffing strip and embroidered insertion, and is finished with a French band. The materials are available from fine sewing shops. This is a good project to expand your knowledge of heirloom sewing.

MATERIALS NEEDED

1/4 yard (.2 m) fabric, cotton or silk
  batiste or fine linen

1 yard (.9 m) cotton lace insertion,
  1/2 inch (13 mm) wide

1/2 yard (.5 m) cotton lace beading,
  5/8 inch (15 mm) wide

3/4 yard (.7 m) cotton lace edging

1/2 yard embroidered cotton insertion,
  5/8 inch wide

1/4 yard embroidered cotton beading,
  1/2 inch wide

3/4 yards entredeux

2 yards (1.8 m) satin ribbon in white
  or contrasting color, 1/4 inch
  (6 mm) wide

Hand sewing needle

Spool of fine thread #50 or #60,
  same color as fabric

Spool of fine thread #50 or #60,
  same color as lace

Sharp scissors

PROCEDURE

1. Prewash and press all materials
   to avoid shrinkage. Cut two
   12-1/2-inch (32 cm) strips of lace
   insertion and one 12-1/2-inch strip
   of embroidered insertion. Set the
   sewing machine on the zigzag stitch
   with the width set to cover the headings of one edge of the lace insertion.
   (See basic instructions.)

2. Zigzag stitch the lace heading of one
   piece of lace insertion to the entredeux edge of the embroidered insertion. (You may substitute a hand or
   machine embroidered strip of insertion with the entredeux attached to
   both sides of the long edge. This
   insertion strip may be attached to
   the lace with the point-de-Paris or
   pin stitch by hand, or by machine
   instead of using the entredeux.)

3. Place the second strip of lace
   insertion on the other side of the
   embroidered insertion and stitch.
   This should result in a 12-1/2-inch
   strip of insertion that is the beginning of the fancy band.

4. Zigzag the piece of embroidered
   beading to one edge of the fancy
   band, which should now be about
   2-1/4 inches (56 mm) wide. Press
   face-down on a padded surface using
   spray sizing. Gather the lace edging
   evenly and zigzag it to the edge of
   the embroidered beading.

5. For the puffing, cut a strip of fabric 2-1/4 inches wide and 25 inches (62 cm) long (or twice as long as the fancy band). Gather both long edges, lining up the gathers evenly on both sides. Attach the puffing to the fancy band with entredeux or pin stitch, and stitch the lace beading to the other side of the puffing.

6. Finish the fancy band ends with a machine roll edge. Stitch across the ends by machine, trim, and then zigzag over the edge.

7. To make the French band, cut a 10-inch (25 cm) bias strip. Cut the ribbon in half. Insert the ribbon through both beading strips and make knots at each end. The ribbon should be able to gather freely, allowing the bonnet to fit a baby or a doll.

Note: The above directions are for a newborn size. For a 6-month size, cut the insertion strips 13-1/2 inches (35 cm) long; for a 1-year size, cut the insertion strips 14-1/2 inches (38 cm) long. Use wider strips of lace and puffing strips to maintain proportions. Actual head sizes may vary at any given age.

Sewing for the Baby
By Mary Stauffer Naylor

14564

THIS dainty batiste cap has a new touch in the eyelet and ribbon trimming across the top.

Coach Pillow Made of a Handkerchief

A BRIDE'S handkerchief in fine drawn-work was made into this first-size baby cap.

14562
A Bib and Dress Yoke Combined

14562
These Bibs are to be Worn With Plain Slips

IN PLANNING an outfit for a new baby elaborate materials are not essentials to the comfort of the little one, but everything should be of good quality and hand made if possible. Featherstitching is much used for trimming the first dresses.

A Comfortable Coach Pillow of Batiste

WE CANNOT supply special patterns for the piqué coat and the sacque, but a baby's coat pattern, No. 5417, price fifteen cents, and a sacque pattern, No. 6915, price ten cents, are similar in style, and could be adapted by the maker.

14562-6344
A Pretty Yoke Design in Featherstitching

14563
Of Twilled Silk With a Thin Silk Lining

5475
A First-Size Nightgown, Opening to the Hem

A Plain Piqué Coat With Dainty Trimmings

THE LADIES' HOME JOURNAL, JANUARY, 1913

ANTIQUE LACE CRAFTS

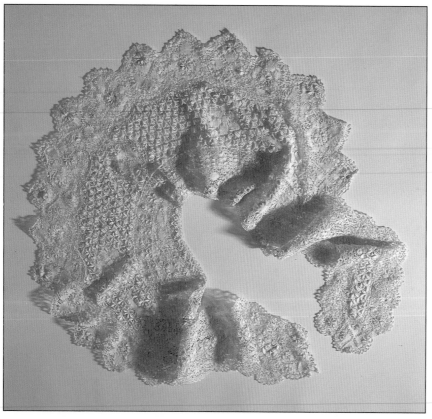

ABOVE: HANDMADE MALTESE BOBBIN LACE, C. 1600

The English word lace has been used to refer to airy, decorative, openwork fabric only since 1555, around the same time that lace making became a commercial effort. Lace is further defined as being made of thread that has been twisted, looped, or knotted by means of a needle, bobbin, hook, or, more recently, by machine. The word lace comes from the Latin word *laques* meaning noose or snare. This meaning is also shared by the old French word *laz*. In France, the word *passements* was used to designate lace in early lists and inventories. Later, *passements dentelles* was employed, until finally *passements* was left off, leaving only *dentelles*, which remains the French word for lace.

Several other terms are commonly used to refer to distinct varieties of lace. *Points*, the French word for stitch, generally refers to needlepoint lace; however, the word is also used to designate lace that is designed with a combination of tapes or braids and needlepoint stitches. *Punto* is the Italian word for needlepoint lace. Large patterned lace motifs with flowing designs can be joined with "brides" or buttonhole stitched bars, and are then generally classified as "guipure" laces. Guipure laces are also characterized by a thick cord or thread that is part of their design.

Bobbin lace is characterized by its delicate patterns of fine thread that have been interlaced or plaited to produce an even or nearly flat surface. It was sometimes called "bone lace" and was worked with spindles (spools or reels wound with thread), which was an early name for bobbin. The early bobbins were often made from sheep bones, as were the pins used to define the lace pattern. Later, in the 16th century, metal pins were developed and bobbins were made of wood.

Pattern areas of bobbin lace evolved with a flowing design connected with mesh or net-like background stitches. Many different types of background stitches were used, and each country developed a distinct twist of its own. Early bobbin lace motifs were attached with a needle-made bride (bars made with buttonhole stitch) ground. Fine, delicate lace patterns were usually connected with a *reseau*, French for background mesh or network. Reseau was made with the needle or in conjunction with the weaving of bobbin lace made on a pillow.

Valenciennes lace was made with varied grounds, and several different styles were often used in one piece of lace. Duchesse lace was made with davonia ground, which was known as *droschel* in Flanders. Mechlin lace was worked with both hexagonal and round droschel. The ground for a large piece of Duchesse lace was made of the finest linen thread plaited in strips that were joined together invisibly by a needle and a single thread. Honiton lace was also made with a distinct background network.

Linen was the primary thread used to create the fine openwork fabric known as lace. Sometimes linen was combined with gold or silver threads when court costumes for the nobility were being made. Silk was also used for these expensive lace embellishments; however, it is

HANDMADE NEEDLEPOINT POINT DE GAZE EDGING FROM 18TH-CENTURY BRUSSELS

linen's durability that may well be responsible for the examples of lace that have survived from Renaissance times.

A special flax fiber was grown in Flanders and used in the very fine linen thread of Brabant (Brussels) for the exquisite and expensive Brussels bobbin lace. The delicate fiber was spun in damp cellars to preserve its strength by only the most experienced women, who took great care to produce a consistent, even strand of the costly thread. Celebrated for both bobbin and needlepoint laces, lace made in Flanders was in great demand all over Europe and especially prized in England, whose native laces were much coarser and therefore less desirable.

Nuns supported their convents by making lace, and they also taught the young girls of the nobility entrusted to their training to make lace. Ladies of the nobility taught those who served them to make cutwork and bobbin lace. The fine cutwork laces made in Western Europe during the Renaissance (c. 1450–1600), were most likely made first in Venice. Bobbin lace may also have originated in Italy; however, it was Flanders that developed the pillow laces.

Flanders was an important textile-producing center during the 13th and 14th centuries, and the major lace-making country in Northern Europe from the Renaissance on. Parts of Flanders were at different times annexed by both France and Spain, which may contribute to the claims of both these countries to being first to make lace. Both France and Spain, as well as England, imported lace made in Flanders during the 16th century. Prior to 1665, most of the beautiful bobbin laces made on pillows in Flanders were known as Malines. Brussels point plat, and Mechlin lace were made by the nuns. Brussels point was worked on a pillow or with the needle, and sometimes a combination of both techniques was used. Other popular needlepoint laces, which were more costly than the bobbin laces, were called Brabant lace, Point de Flandre, Point d'Aguille, Point Gaze, and Point d'Angleterre.

Bruges, the great commercial city of Northern Europe, was (and remains) an important textile center, as well as a major city of the Flanders lace-making industry during the Renaissance. A Mechlin lace similar to the French Valenciennes and the highly valued guipure de Bruges were both made and exported in great quantities.

Most of the lace makers were women; however, both girls and boys were taught at a very early age to make bobbin lace, and men would sometimes sit down to a pillow in the evening after their regular day's work was finished.

There were several ways of making the early bobbin lace. A strip of tape or braid was made on a pillow for the first method. This tape or braid strip was usually the first bobbin lace made by a beginning lace crafter, as it required fewer bobbins and a simpler pattern with frequent repeats. The completed lengths of tape or braid were then laid out on a fabric or parchment pattern so the background stitches could be worked, usually by more experienced lace makers. Sometimes the tape or braid was attached to a net or meshlike background that had been worked as a separate strip of bobbin lace.

When a large or wide piece of lace was required, such as for a full skirt or bedcover, the motifs and ground were made separately by many workers who each completed individual motifs. When all the motifs were completed, they were attached to the net ground by hand with tiny, invisible stitches. Usually the net ground was cut away under the motifs. Floral motifs were popular, but animals, birds, emblems, initials, and even people appeared on the pillows of the lace makers. Point de Flandre or Brussels lace was made this way with its large floral motifs. Duchesse lace is another variety of this type of bobbin lace. The English Honiton lace with smaller pattern designs was also derived from this method of Brussels lace.

Another technique employed by advanced lace makers was to weave the design and back-

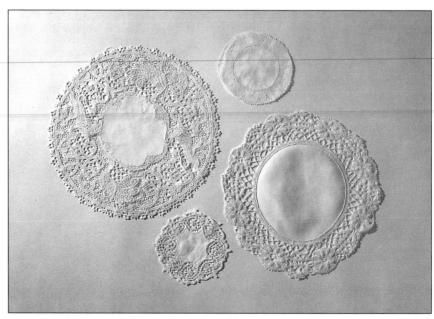

ENGLISH HONITON DOILY, TOP LEFT, AND SEVERAL BOBBIN LACE DOILIES FROM THE EARLY 1800s

ground stitches of the ground at the same time around pins stuck in a pattern drawn on parchment that had been fastened to a pillow. The pillows were set in stands or held on the laps of the lace makers, who were usually women. Experienced lace makers often handled more than a hundred pairs of bobbins to create complicated patterns and worked for many hours to make a single length of lace. The lace could be worked with two straight edges for lace insertion, or a scalloped edge could be added to one side for lace edging or wide flounce.

The lace makers recited story/chants called "tells" as they worked long hours over their pillows. The tells helped the work go faster as the bobbins flew. When they slowed down or fell behind in the expected production, a period of silence called a "glum" was imposed. As soon as the work was caught up, the lace makers could again recite their legends of romance, bloodshed, or scary spirits.

Royalty wore the ornate laces for court presentations and celebrations. Indeed, lace was so expensive that only the very wealthy could afford to wear it. Costly and precious, lace was considered an appropriate and very

special gift for a king to give his bride. Beyond personal enjoyment, kings and queens wore lace (and required their courtiers to wear it as well) in support of their countries' lace industries. There were three well-known 16th-century queens who were especially influential in starting lace making as an industry in France and England.

Catherine de Medicis (1519-1589), queen of France, who conveyed the lace making skills of Italian noblewomen to the ladies of the French court, is generally credited with establishing France's lace making tradition. Catherine was sumptuously dressed in lace and surrounded herself with a lace-bedecked nobility. Much of the ladies' time at court was passed with needle and bobbins making the lace collars and ruffs (fluted neck ruffles) and sleeve and boot ruffles that decorated the ornate courtiers' costumes. Even the boots and shoes were embellished with lace rosettes. Importing large quantities of expensive lace from Italy during the 16th century, France set the styles of courtly fashion that were followed by the rest of Europe.

Katherine of Aragon, the first wife of Henry VIII, shared the lace making skills of Spain with the skilled Anglo-Saxon needle women of the English court as well as the women outside the palace walls. Katherine is credited with teaching the peasants around Bedfordshire and Buckingham which gave them a means of economic support to improve their lives and also began the English lace-making industry.

Queen Elizabeth I of England (1533–1603), the daughter of Henry VIII and Anne Boleyn, was more interested in affairs of state than in making lace. However, she did lead the style for the wider and more elaborate neck ruffles that were popular during her reign. Starched and fluted, the ornate lace-trimmed neck ruffles became wider and more ornate in imitation of Queen Elizabeth. She received many gifts of fans and other fine laces, which she enjoyed wearing to embellish her many ornate be-jeweled costumes throughout her long reign from 1558 to 1603.

By wearing lace, she supported and helped the lace making industry flourish in England.

So great was the demand for lace in England that the convents and noblewomen could not supply enough—even with the help of the peasants. England's lace industry was more firmly established during the mid-17th century with some indirect assistance from the Protestant reformation of Northern Europe. The reformation was responsible for many of the Catholic lace workers of Flanders emigrating to England to escape religious persecution. They quickly reestablished themselves and their lace making arts. Since higher wages were paid for lace making than other trades, workers eagerly produced the precious lace that contributed to the overall economy of 16th-century England.

Sumptuary Laws—laws designed to limit the amount of money spent on lace and on foreign purchases—severely limited the production of gold and silver lace, but did not seem to have much effect on the wearing of all laces, especially those made of linen thread. Italy, France, and England all issued these regulations, which were strictly enforced in Italy but almost ignored in France and England. Smuggling became a major activity to offset the edicts against lace importation.

So great was the English desire for Brussels lace, that great quantities were smuggled into England under the name of point d'Angleterre. The Courts of James I, from 1603–1625, and his son Charles I, from 1625-1649, were resplendent with lace. Civil war and the execution of Charles I in 1649 deposed the Royal House of Stuart and signaled a temporary end to sumptuous personal adornment in the British Isles. When the Puritans (under the leadership of Oliver Cromwell) gained power, the falling collars made fashionable during the early 1600s were worn without the magnificent lace trims. Later, in 1660, the monarchy was restored under Charles II, and the wearing of lace at court resumed.

Meanwhile, across the English channel, France began a period of high living that resulted in the production of magnificent needlepoint laces, which greatly affected the French economy. Italy, Spain, and France created many variations of the basic buttonhole stitch to produce the elegant needlepoint laces of the 17th and 18th centuries. Accompanying the extravagant laces of the courtiers' costumes were beautiful silks produced in France. Although few examples of these wondrous silks have survived, the treasured laces were carefully removed from the silk gowns for later generations to inherit.

During the reign of Henry IV, from 1589–1610, laws were issued in France to lessen the abuse of wearing lace by the nobility, who often lost their fortunes in an attempt to satisfy their cravings for lace. Trying to prevent such excessive and compulsive behavior, another law was issued in 1629, by the stricter Louis XIII, who ruled from 1610–1643. This edict was called "The Regulation as to Superfluity in Costume," and was also virtually ignored. Although affected by the sumptuary laws, lace making had been a major support of the women in central France at Le Puy Centre from the 15th century, and they were not about to relinquish this source of income.

Additional centres were developed in the 17th century, and the French lace making industry was firmly established by the 1640s. The laces made in the centres of Aurillac, Sedan, Reims, le Quesnoy, Alençon, Arras, Loudan, and others were generally referred to as points de France. Villum (or Alençon centre point lace) was a needlepoint lace worked on geometric parchment patterns as early as 1615. Adaptations of Venetian point and the Points d'Argentan and de Bruxelles as well as point d'Angleterre originated for court dress during the reign of Louis XIII. The need for some control over the lace-wearing mania among the nobles is clearly revealed by an inventory in 1642 of the estate of Cinq Mars, which included "300 sets collars and cuffs trimmed with lace."

Louis XIV (called "le Grande") established a resplendent dress code requiring that lace be worn at the palaces in Paris and Versailles. In order to satisfy the elaborate tastes of the French court, France imported much of the fine laces used from Flanders and Italy, especially the lovely Venetian point. Louis XIV recognized the economic necessity for producing the required laces within France. During his long reign from 1643–1715, he expanded the silk and lace making industries of France under the capable direction of his Minister of France, Jean Baptiste Colbert.

Colbert set up the Alençon and other lace making industries to keep the money spent on imported laces within the economy of France. While the French convents and the poor supported themselves making needlepoint lace, the Villum or point de France lace did not approach the delicacy and intricacy of Venetian point. Designs for many of the patterns of lace ordered from other countries were frequently created by the French. They also set the styles of the court costumes worn all over 17th-century Europe, so it seemed reasonable that the laces could be domestically produced. Colbert visited the areas in France that were producing lace and sent the daughters of the lace makers to Venice, Italy, to learn the art of making Venetian point. When the lace makers returned, Alençon lace produced at Alençon Centre was created similar to Venetian point with gracefully flowing flowers and scrolls on a net ground, replacing the earlier geometric patterns.

The Alençon lace industry was officially organized in August of 1665, with headquarters in the Hotel de Beaufort in Paris. Colbert brought 30 lace makers from Italy and 200 from Flanders to assist the French. Lace makers earned high wages, and soon there were 1600 French girls producing the beautiful Alençon lace.

Fashion dolls or *poupees* dressed in the finest of French silks and laces were instrumental in spreading the new styles to Italy, Vienna, and England. Dolls as tall as 4 feet (3.6 m) were dressed in *La Mode* and sent as emissaries on behalf of France's lace and fashion industries. The countries receiving the dolls copied the new fashions decreed by France, which hoped that they would also import the silks and fine French laces to reproduce the clothing exactly as exhibited.

Large quantities of Valenciennes bobbin lace trimmings were made from about 1650, and were widely used for ordinary occasions. Less expensive as well as easier to make than the needlepoint laces they competed with, Valenciennes was an important part of the clothing of the lower classes.

Louis XIV also encouraged the production of Valenciennes lace in the Flemish towns of Hainault that had been acquired by France. Valenciennes was made in several cities in the lace making area around Brussels, as well as in France. Between 1720 and 1780, more than 14,000 Valenciennes lace makers worked on their pillows to produce the popular lace trimmings with a twisted ground and flat pattern areas.

During the early 18th century jabots (cravats or "falling frills") replaced the "falling collars" of 17th-century male attire. Gentlemen wore flowing, curled hairstyles and wigs as well as less lace, while women increased their passion for lace by wearing more. Full skirts exhibited layer upon filmy layer of wide lace flounces, with more flounces at the neckline and sleeves of the

18th-century lady. The earlier, large floral lace patterns were replaced by small blossoms scattered over a net ground, resulting in lighter needlepoint laces with more detail.

Venetian needlepoint lace remained somewhat formal in design; however, the French and Flemish laces were filmy and playful. Brussels' lace makers replaced the heavy, sculptural pattern outline (or cordonnet) with a lighter thread of low relief. The ornate needlepoint laces were so expensive and difficult to make that only the very rich could afford to wear them, and the less costly bobbin laces became fashionable. The laces and styles worn reflected the ever-more-frivolous lifestyle of the French court. Reception of courtiers was no longer limited to the formal rooms, and had moved to bedrooms resplendent with lace during the reign of Louis XV, king of France from 1715 to 1774.

The reign of Louis XV is marked by the production of Chantilly blonde lace, which was made of both black and white silk threads, beginning in 1740. A luxurious pillow lace, it was made at Caen and Bayeux as well as Chantilly Centre. Later, around 1745, blonde lace of unbleached silk threads was produced in Barcelona and Catelonia, Spain. These blonde laces were charac-

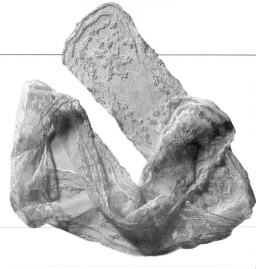

terized by solid floral patterns united by a mesh ground. While they appear heavier than needlepoint laces, blonde (and especially Chantilly blonde) laces are soft and filmy, perfect for the full skirts and gathered flounces of the time. Due to extravagance and poor leadership, France lost a great deal of the empire amassed by Louis XV's predecessors, and the country, along with its Sovereign, faced financial ruin.

Louis XVI, who ruled from 1774 to 1792, along with his unpopular queen, Marie Antoinette, continued the lifestyle of fantastic excess at court, despite the lack of funds to pay for it. Less expensive than needlepoint laces, Chantilly blonde laces were worn by Marie-Antoinette and were displayed a great deal at court. The Chantilly blondes remained in style until the French Revolution destroyed the lace makers at Chantilly and the French lace industry, along with the hated monarchs.

Linen thread was made in

Flanders and Ireland, silk in France, and wool in England. By the late 1600s, cotton, which was called "cotton wool" or "brushed wool," was spun by machine in England. Easier to grow, cotton was less expensive than linen. The short staple cotton fiber was grown in India and imported into England, but the short fibers of this cotton were hard to spin. Richard Arkwright of Nottingham, England, received a patent in 1769 for a "machine making Cotton into Yarn." Horses supplied the strength to run his water frame and spin long lengths of thread from raw fiber.

Sea Island cotton, a fine long staple fiber, was introduced for lace making around 1770. Linen thread was used for much of the lace produced before 1800; however, many laces of the late 18th and early 19th centuries were made with fine cotton thread. England imported Sea Island cotton from the American colonies, where it was grown in Georgia and Florida.

Scotland soon manufactured fine cotton lace thread on 500 machines, with each machine requiring 36 people to operate it. White thread lace and black silk lace were produced on a loom developed by Mr. Brotherton of Leith, Scotland, as early as 1775. This loom produced an inexpensive early bobbin net as well as lace that imitated patterns from 3 to 27 inches (7 to 67 cm) wide.

Besides lace, Valenciennes also produced large quantities of stockings. As early as 1615, stocking frame machines were imported from England, where they had originated in 1589. Stocking frames were also sent to Italy. Between 1670 and 1695, 400 frames were shipped to Valenciennes, France, and Italy. Weavers experimented with the stocking frames to develop a lace-making machine that would produce net or tulle. A stocking frame was adapted by Hammond in 1768, who made lace caps similar to the bobbin lace produced by his wife.

Hammond's net was a "point" or "pin" net woven or looped with a single thread. Snagging or pulling the single thread could result in a run that would ruin the net. Other net patterns were soon made including "barley corn," "square," and "spider" net. The machines were not perfected to produce tulle and lace until the beginning of the 19th century.

Napoleon Bonaparte emerged from the revolution as the leader of France and was crowned Emperor in 1804. Legal freedom and reunion with the Catholic church marked his reign. Re-building France, Napoleon attempted to reestablish the lace industry in 1905, especially Alençon, Bruxelles, and Chantilly. All light laces, they complemented the sheer silk and muslin (linen) fabrics of the simple classical styles of the early 19th century. Lace cravats tied at the throat were worn by men.

Bees, the symbol of Napoleon I, decorated the ground of Alençon lace bed hangings and coverlets, as well as a shawl ordered for his wife, Marie-Louise. The lace shawls exhibiting the bee ground with a decorative border were worn with simple muslin gowns. Valenciennes lace in narrow widths for insertions and edgings also enjoyed a revival; however, the costly and heavier needlepoint laces did not regain favor.

Many improvements to the stocking frame with warp attachments

ABOVE: MACHINE-MADE CHANTILLY LACE DRESS WITH A HANDMADE SILK THREAD OUTLINE FROM THE 1800s

OPPOSITE PAGE: HANDMADE BOBBIN LACE SCARF

were tried to produce a net that would imitate the ground of bobbin lace. During the early 1800s, a fine tulle net ground was made by machine, and in 1808, John Heathcoat finally produced an acceptable cotton thread, two-twist bobbin-net on his machine, "Old Loughborough." The bobbin-net machine replaced the necessity for long hours of handwork to produce the ground, since the handmade bobbin lace

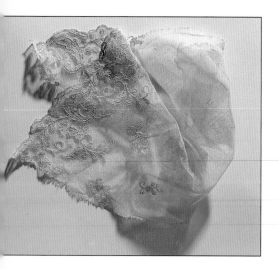

late 1830s and early 1840s.

Laces made by machine were called "imitation" lace as they copied or imitated the patterns and designs of the "real" laces. Because they were mass-produced of cotton thread, the machine-made laces were comparatively inexpensive and available for the fashionable dresses worn by 19th-century ladies. Tapes or braids were also produced, including several kinds of Honiton braid. An English "straight-bolt" lace machine, along with the workers to operate it, was set up at Calais in 1817–19. Calais lace makers produced imitation bobbin lace of the Malines and Valenciennes varieties. Another nearby town of northern France produced Lille and Chantilly laces.

motifs could be stitched directly to the tulle. By the 1820s, circular, pusher, and Levers Lleavers) machines were advanced to the point where they were able to reproduce—by the thousands of yards—the bobbin laces that earlier had taken hundreds and sometimes thousands of hours to make by hand. Jacquard improvements were added to the warp frames to produce laces with designs woven into the net. Further jacquard improvements to the pusher and levers machines were made in the

The industrial age embraced the laces made by machine; however, "real" handmade lace was still in demand by the affluent ladies of the 19th century, who prided themselves on their capacity to exhibit the pricey luxury. They prompted a resurgence in the craft of handmade lace; however, the new technology was incorporated into the handmade laces. Machine-made net was often used for the background of handmade sprigs of bobbin lace motifs. Needlepoint stitches were also applied to the net grounds, and combinations of fabric and net were created.

Irish carrickmacross, an appliqué lace on net ground, was made around 1820. The Italian needle-point laces influenced the design of the new carrickmacross, which was produced by the Irish con-

UPPER LEFT: MACHINE-MADE NET THAT'S BEEN HAND EMBROIDERED FROM THE EARLY 1800s

LOWER LEFT: MACHINE-MADE NET COLLAR THAT'S BEEN HAND EMBROIDERED FROM THE 1830s

ABOVE: HANDMADE HONITON POINT AND APPLIQUÉ LACE COLLAR FROM THE MID-1800s

UPPER RIGHT: EMBROIDERED MACHINE-MADE NET DRESSER SCARF AND INSERTION FROM THE 1850s

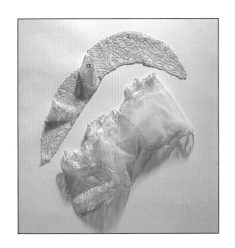

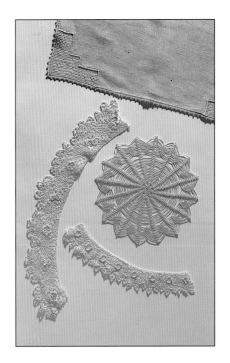

The failure of Ireland's potato crop in 1846 marked the beginning of Irish needlepoint lace, which was

vents. Various tools were used to make Irish lace. About 1829, tambour embroidery, which originated in the eastern countries of Persia, China, India, and Turkey, was worked with a chain stitch on net ground.

influenced by point de Venice. Irish crochet, worked with a hook

🍃 CARE AND REUSE OF ANTIQUE LACE TREASURES 🍃

Lucky the lady who inherits antique lace or finds a treasure in an antique or collectibles shop. Antique laces can be reused many times, indeed by the time the precious lace comes into your possession it may have enjoyed several previous lives. Lace can be removed from old garments—even if the garment is in shreds—and then washed and reused. Whether these precious antique laces will survive and be enjoyed by future generations depends a great deal on the care it receives now.

The first consideration is the age of the lace. The photographs in this book may assist you in identification. There are a number of other books available, with many recent reprints of historic editions available to assist in determining the age and variety of antique lace. Further reference sources are listed in the bibliography. Museums with antique lace collections are another resource for dating laces. If your lace is very old or unusual, the curator of a museum collection may be able to help you.

Laces made before 1800 might better be taken out from their place of storage, enjoyed for a few minutes, and then returned to a dry, safe area. Lace produced by hand or machine

CONTINUED ON PAGE 65

and a single ball of thread without any net background, soon developed, adapted from Venetian rose point by the Carmelite convent. Irish crochet soon spread to convents all over Ireland, and Irish immigrants brought this lace craft to the United States. Easy-to-make crocheted lace has remained popular.

Fashion styles reverted to wide full skirts and narrow waistlines during the 1830s, echoing the elegance of the French court of Marie Antoinette. When Victoria was crowned Queen of England in 1837, she inspired fashion to return to wearing her beloved laces. She wore handmade (even to the net ground) English Honiton lace to celebrate her marriage to the German Prince Albert in 1840. Queen Victoria continued to wear the precious laces from her wedding at the baptisms of their nine children, as well as other special family occasions. After the death of

Prince Albert in 1870, she wore black mourning for the rest of her life, including the black lace shawls so popular with 19th-century ladies.

White, black, and ecru laces made by machine were produced in large quantities for the fashionable lace-embellished gowns worn by the ladies of the mid-19th century. Wide flounces of machine-made Mechlin and Chantilly laces adorned the ball gowns of the ladies, who carried large handkerchiefs edged with Valenciennes and Honiton lace. Basques (jackets), mantillas, shawls and fichus, chemisettes (partial blouses worn under day dresses), collars, jabots,

bonnets, cuffs and sleeve ruffles, removable sleeves, neck ruffles, parasols, and fans were all made entirely or adorned with lace. Infant christening dresses as well as children's dresses were also trimmed with lace. The lace cravats worn by men in the early 19th century were made from muslin or silk and trimmed with lace or embroidery.

Lingerie was also embellished with lace. Nightgowns and negligées, corset covers or camisoles, pantaloons, and petticoats were all personal items to be lavished with the lovely laces. Lace was primarily decorative; however, there was a practical side to using it so profusely in the 19th century. Edgings on the bottom of petticoats often dragged in the mud or were caught in a heel. Lace edgings were easily replaced or added on a garment that would otherwise have to be discarded. Lace was frequently added to seams of dresses, especially when the wearer's size increased beyond the capacity of the tucks and seams to be let out.

Exhibitions of the finest laces and other manufactured products were held in European and English countries throughout the 19th century. Alençon lace was shown in the Exhibition of 1851, helping to give new life to the industry. An Alençon flounce that required "thirty-six women, eighteen months to complete" and was valued at 22,000 francs, later became a part of the wedding finery of the Empress Eugenie. Eugenie wore the beautiful French and Brussels laces during the second empire of France (1853–1870). Many of her gowns, resplendent with lace, were made by the couturier Charles Worth, and both black and white laces were favored. The black Chantilly lace shawls in triangular shapes were introduced at this time. While a few were of handmade lace, machine-made

NEAR RIGHT: DETAIL OF THE SHAWL SHOWN OPPOSITE PAGE, TOP, WITH A HANDMADE EMBROIDERED OUTLINE

TOP RIGHT: MACHINE-MADE NEEDLEPOINT LACE COLLARS FROM THE LATE 1800s

copies were soon worn everywhere.

The custom of dressing French fashion dolls, which had been discontinued with the French Revolution, was now revived by the couturiers. These dolls were sent all over the world to spread the news of French fashions and laces and were eagerly received in America, where orders for full-sized gowns

replicating the dolls' were sent back across the Atlantic.

Chantilly, Alençon, and other laces with an outline or raised cordonnet around the pattern utilized machine-made background lace. The pattern was then outlined by hand-stitched thread on the sewing machines used by the lace industry at this time. Although the marvelous steam-powered machines were able to closely reproduce the bobbin lace

between 1800 and 1880 may have very fine thread and be very fragile. Reuse of these pieces should be undertaken with great care. The antique Victorian blouse (page 75) and both collar projects (pages 69 and 82) included in this section have reused lace made circa 1880.

Lace from the late 19th and early 20th centuries is plentiful, and much of it is in good and reusable condition. These are the laces you will most likely find in antique and collectibles shops. Most of the photographs of antique laces included in this book are from this period in history.

Lace tends to mildew and rot when kept in damp conditions, so a warm, dry storage area is very important in preservation. Lace-work on linen fabric still in recognizable condition was found in ancient Egyptian tombs that are more than 4,000 years old. Pure cotton or linen fabric is recommended for storage bags and wrappings. Special archival boxes and tissue are also available to help preserve antique lace, historic garments, and household linens.

Antique lace may be stained and spotted with rust or mildew. Washing with a mild soap like Orvus Paste (available from most feed and grain suppliers because it's used for bathing animals) should remove most grease and many other stains. Wearing plastic or rubber gloves is recommended to protect the lace from snags. Soaking for several hours will allow the fibers to release the soil. The water should not contain chlorine or any other additives like fluoride

CONTINUED ON PAGE 67

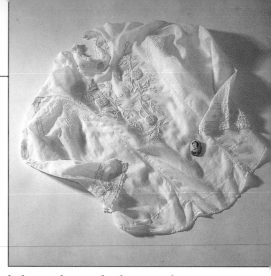

patterns, the needlepoint laces were more difficult. Using a side-to-side satin stitch, the needle-point patterns were adapted for the machines; however, an actual

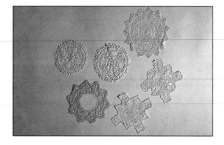

buttonhole stitch was not reproduced during the 19th century.

Lace curtains were made on the lace machines, especially at Nottingham, where 2,448 machines were busily at work in 1862. The same year there were 3,552 lace machines altogether in England alone! A vital part of Victorian decor, doilies, bedspreads, and tablecloths were also made on the lace machines at Nottingham.

More tailored styles for women's clothing were introduced in the 1880s: skirts with jackets or suits were the fashionable daytime look

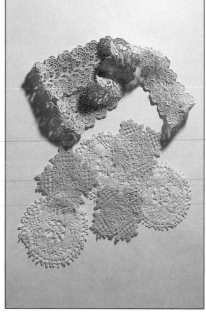

as women began to venture into the business world. Chemisettes were worn under the jackets, and by the 1890s, blouses complete with sleeves and high collars (the Russian look) became the perfect base for lace embellishment. Ball gowns, especially those designed by Charles Worth and other Paris couturiers, continued to be embellished with lace.

Gracious and softly feminine lingerie dresses with lace insertions and edgings, which had earlier been worn only at home, were now called tea gowns. These gowns were worn on Sundays and regular daytime occasions in the summertime by the end of the 19th century. The

lightweight muslin linen and cotton fabric dresses were often made by young ladies who were justifiably proud of their accomplishments with the needle. The beautiful dresses were also worn for graduations and weddings. Later, they were carefully wrapped and stored, along with other laces, as treasured memories. Many of these dresses have survived and are being rediscovered.

The 19th century was called the Victorian Age in honor of the

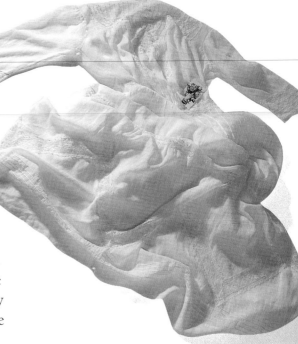

diminutive queen, whose influences and power spread throughout the British Empire and thus the whole world. The British brought the lace industry to all of the countries within the great empire, including China and India. Lace making had spread all over the civilized world, including South America and Brazil, where it was an important industry. Victoria's long life ended in January of 1901, allowing her son Edward to assume the crown of the great empire. Styles in the Edwardian age continued to be adorned with lace held over from the Victorians. Lingerie dresses and tea gowns remained in fashion throughout the Edwardian age, which lasted until 1911.

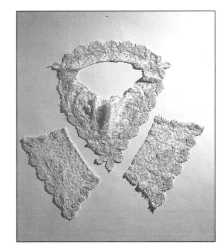

Styles became narrow to a point of tripping the ladies who wore them, as hobble skirts became the rage. Less lace appeared on the tailored dresses and suits of ladies of the World War I era, but blouses and collars and cuffs with lace trim continued to be worn throughout the early years of the 20th century. Most of the antique lace collars and cuffs were put away for future use

RIGHT: CUFFS AND COLLARS FROM THE 1920s

OPPOSITE PAGE, LOWER LEFT: NOTTINGHAM LACE FROM THE 1900s

OPPOSITE PAGE, UPPER LEFT: IMITATION BOBBIN LACE DOILIES; MACHINE-MADE NEEDLEPOINT DOILIES FROM THE LATE 1800s TO EARLY 1900s.

OPPOSITE PAGE, CENTER: MACHINE IMITATION BOBBIN LACE DOILIES; MACHINE-MADE NEEDLEPOINT DOILIES FROM THE LATE 1800s TO EARLY 1900s.

OPPOSITE PAGE, UPPER RIGHT: LACE INSERTION BLOUSE WITH RUSSIAN-STYLE COLLAR, C. 1890

OPPOSITE PAGE, LOWER RIGHT: LINGERIE DRESS, C. 1900

because they may stain the lace or destroy the fibers. Distilled water is advised if your water system contains added chemicals or if it naturally includes rust or minerals that make it hard. Special products are available for removing rust stains. Chlorine bleach should never be used to remove stains.

Rinsing well is very important because soap left in the fibers tends to destroy the lace over a period of time. Rinsing in a clear glass bowl will help you determine when the water is completely clear. Ten rinses is a minimum, and some laces need twice that many rinses. When thoroughly rinsed, set the lace on a terry towel to drain the excess water. NEVER wring out antique lace!

If the lace is still stained, dyeing with tan dye or coffee or tea may be desirable. The coffee imparts a warm tone, while the tea gives a cooler shade of ecru. Test small pieces to determine the color before going ahead with the entire lace. As with soap, all residue of the dye must be rinsed away or it may destroy the fibers.

Lay the still wet lace on a dry terry towel on a flat surface. Carefully smooth the lace with your fingertips, straightening the edges and patterns as you go. Hours later, the dry lace should be smooth or nearly so, and may be stored without ironing. Antique lace should

CONTINUED ON PAGE 68

when the bias cut dresses of the 1930s came into style. Evening gowns, lingerie, and children's clothes were embellished with lace, while bridal finery of the 20th century included as much or even more lace. Women continued to make cutwork and needlepoint lace, as well as crocheted and tatted laces for their homes and for gifts. Lace in men's

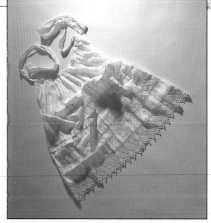

fashions, however, completely disappeared after the turn of the century.

World War I and II soldiers and sailors purchased Valenciennes lace-edged handkerchiefs and pillows for their sweethearts back home. These lace gifts from abroad helped to revive the war-

ravaged European lace industry and created a renewed interest in the machine-made patterns of the exquisite antique laces. The handkerchiefs and pillows were also tucked away to be taken out once in a while, along with the memories of long ago.

FAR LEFT: TATTING, C. 1930

CENTER: NORWEGIAN CROCHETED APRON, C. 1920

ABOVE: VALENCIENNES LACE PILLOW AND HANDKERCHIEF, 1918, 1919

be pressed gently, face down, and then only if needed for reuse.

This chapter of antique lace crafts should help you decide how to reuse your treasured laces. Collars, cuffs, handkerchiefs, and jabots are the most frequently available antique lace items that can be easily incorporated into your current wardrobe. Since they were usually just basted onto garments—so they could be removed and laundered with ease—they are more likely to be in good, reusable condition. Basting them in place or fastening a collar or jabot with an antique brooch, beauty pin or cameo, should help you care for them so they may be passed on to future antique lace lovers.

Repairing antique lace is a true test of a fine needlewoman's skill. Thread that matches the antique thread is absolutely required! Re-stitching an edging of lace to a piece of garment fabric may be easily accomplished using the heirloom sewing techniques discussed earlier. Repairing lace requires matching the twist or plait of the threads, so it's more difficult and time consuming. Practicing on a small piece or section of a garment hidden from view is recommended. It is possible to replace a flower or leaf with one cut from another section of the lace, blending the new stitches in with the old. However, you may prefer to entrust this highly skilled operation to a professional restorer. Museum curators can often recommend someone with the necessary skills to repair a special piece of antique lace.

This collar is the first of two designed to be worn with the antique lace blouse on page 75. Experience with heirloom sewing is needed for this project, so you may want to practice the stitches and techniques beginning on page 14 before you begin. If desired, reproduction lace may be substituted for the antique lace.

MATERIALS NEEDED

1/3 yard (.3 m) fabric, Irish handkerchief linen or fine cotton batiste

30-inch (75 cm) length of lace insertion, 1-1/4 inch (32 mm) wide

10-inch (25 cm) length of lace insertion, 2-1/4 inches (5 cm) wide

2 yards (1.8 m) lace edging, 3/4 to 1 inch (20 to 25 mm) wide

1-1/4 yard (1.1 m) entredeux

1/2 yard (.5 m) lace beading

1 yard (.9 m) narrow silk or satin ribbon

Hand sewing needle

Fine cotton thread #50 or #60

Appliqué scissors

Spray sizing

PROCEDURE

1. Place the pattern on the fabric's fold and cut out the collar. Straight stitch about 1/8 inch (3 mm) from the edge all around the collar. Machine roll the neck's edge. Trim the seam close to the line of stitches, and then zigzag over the edge. Trim threads.

2. Place the collar on a flat, well-padded surface, and press with sizing and a medium-temperature iron. Pin the inside edge only of the 2-1/4-inch lace insertion at both sides of the front opening with the lace placed over the fabric.

3. Gather the 1-1/4-inch lace insertion by pulling the large thread or sewing a gathering thread in the lace header. Pin the ungathered lace edge to the lower edge of the collar. Ease the fullness, and then baste the gathered header of the lace to the fabric. The wider insertion at the front should overlap the narrow insertion around the collar's lower edge. (The fabric will be cut away after the insertion has been machine stitched.)

4. Set the sewing machine to a narrow zigzag stitch and sew the lace to the fabric along the headers of both lace insertions. Trim away the fabric from underneath the lace, taking care not to cut the stitches or lace. Attach both laces by stitching the wider insertion at the front opening all the way down to the collar's lower edge. Straight stitch, then zigzag, across the cut edge of the wider insertion to finish.

5. Point-de-Paris (pin stitch) along the lace insertion where it has been attached to the fabric. This can be done by hand if your sewing machine does not have a pin stitch, or you can eliminate this step.

6. Attach a twin needle to the sewing machine and stitch a decorative pin tuck or regular pin tuck about 1/4 inch (6 mm) from the insertion. Place the collar with the top side face-down on a padded surface. Spray with sizing and press with an iron setting appropriate for the lace.

7. Trim one side of the entredeux, and zigzag it to both edges of the lace insertion at the front opening. Adjust the stitch length so that the needle enters each hole once. Extend the entredeux 1/2 inch (13 mm) below the lace's edge. Attach the entredeux across the lower edge of the insertion, extending 1/2 inch at the corner. Match the holes at the corner and trim the other side of the entredeux.

8. Gather the lace edging. With right sides of the lace edging and insertion together, distribute the gathers evenly and baste to the insertion so that the heading of the lace edging meets the entredeux holes.

9. Turn the collar over so the entredeux is on top and zigzag the lace edging to the entredeux. This step may be done by hand with a whip stitch. Gently pull the lace edging so it's flat. The holes of the entredeux should be open with a zigzag stitch attaching the lace. Gather the lace edging at the neck edge of each side by hand and tack to the insertion edge.

10. Pin the lace beading to the neck edge, and sew with a narrow zigzag stitch to the neck's edge. Fold under at the opening and tack by hand. Press carefully as directed in step 6. Thread the ribbon through the beading and tie to close at the center front. Note: The beading and ribbon may be turned under to conceal if desired, and the bow would then be covered with a brooch.

71

EMERALD LACE SAMPLER

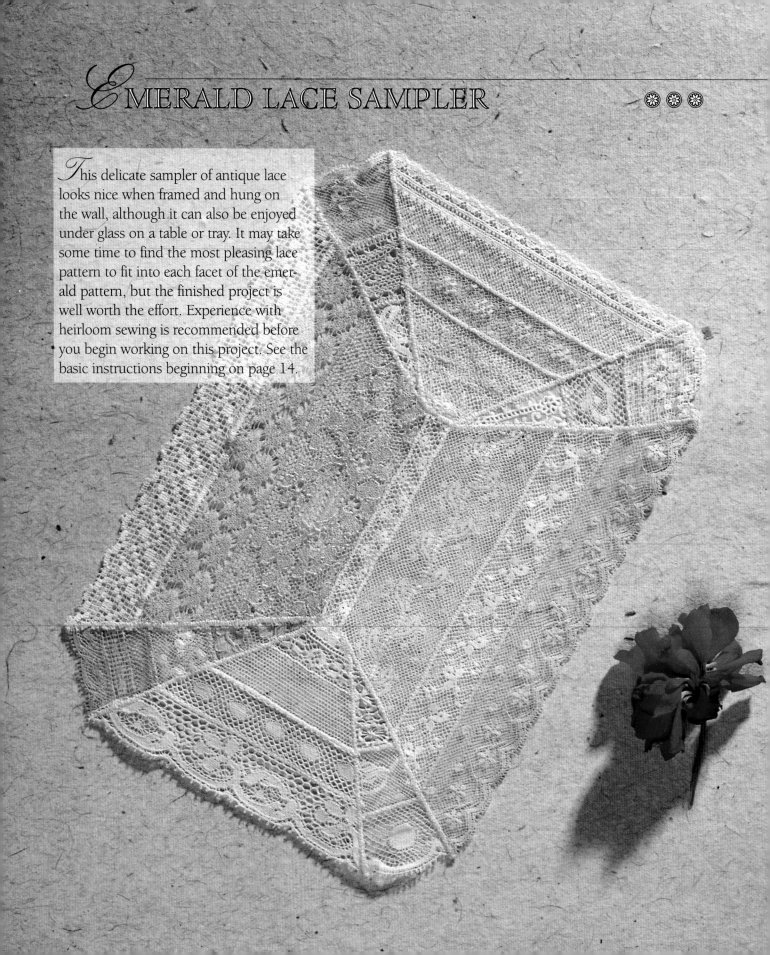

This delicate sampler of antique lace looks nice when framed and hung on the wall, although it can also be enjoyed under glass on a table or tray. It may take some time to find the most pleasing lace pattern to fit into each facet of the emerald pattern, but the finished project is well worth the effort. Experience with heirloom sewing is recommended before you begin working on this project. See the basic instructions beginning on page 14.

MATERIALS NEEDED

12 patterns of lace insertion, 5/8 to 3/4 inch (15 to 20 mm) wide

4 to 8 patterns of lace insertion, 1-1/4 to 1-1/2 inches (32 to 38 mm) wide

1 center pattern of lace insertion, 4 inches (10 cm) long and 3/8 inch (10 mm) wide

8 patterns of lace edging, 1 to 1-1/4 inches (25 to 32 mm) wide

Water-soluble transparent stabilizer

Spool of fine cotton thread #50 or #60

Hand sewing needle

Appliqué scissors

PROCEDURE

1. Wash all laces. Spread them on terry towels to dry and gently finger press them in place. Press lightly and carefully with an iron if needed. Trace the emerald pattern onto the stabilizer with the washable pen. (Blue seems easier to see, but other colors are acceptable.)

2. Pin the lace pieces together on the sides and ends of the pattern, leaving the corners open for now. Narrow insertions can be combined to form wider insertions to fit the emerald's facets.

3. Set the sewing machine for a zigzag stitch that's wide enough to cover the narrow headings of the antique lace insertion. Stitch the sides and center sections using the lace/lace method, and then stitch the two end sections. (See illustration.)

4. Baste the three lace sections to the stabilizer, extending each piece into the corner facet so that the stitching line will be completely covered by lace. Straight stitch on the sewing machine from the end of the center strip to the corner for each side and end facet. (See illustration.)

5. Carefully trim the excess lace along the stitching line. Cut the stabilizer out of the corner sections, leaving the lace sides and ends attached to the stabilizer.

6. Working from the back of the sampler, match the corner laces with the sides and ends sections. Baste; then machine stitch the corners in place, sewing over the previous stitching on the right side of the sampler.

7. Trim the excess corner lace on the back side of the sampler. Zigzag on the right side of the sampler, covering the lines previously straight-stitched. Remove the stabilizer by carefully tearing or cutting it away from the lace.

8. Press the sampler with its right side facing down on a well-padded surface. Cover the lace with a piece of wax paper to absorb the excess

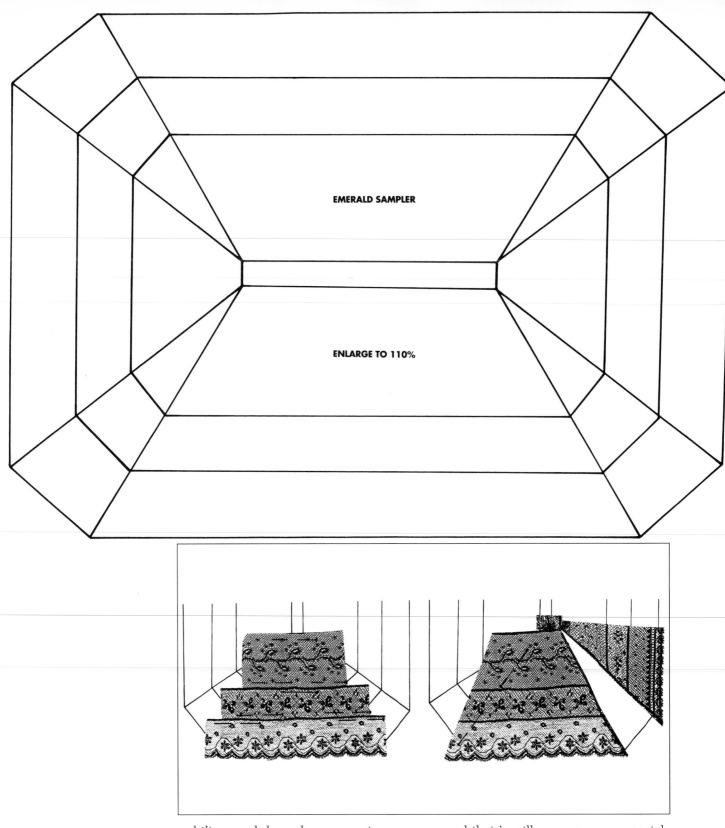

EMERALD SAMPLER

ENLARGE TO 110%

stabilizer, and then place a pressing cloth over the wax paper. Carefully remove the wax paper from the lace while it's still warm to prevent sticking. Press the lace again with a little spray sizing if needed.

Antique Lace Blouse

⊛ ⊛

This beautiful Victorian-styled blouse was inspired by one shown in the October, 1894, issue of the Butterick magazine "The Delineator." During the 1890s, elaborate, lacy blouses were worn with five gored skirts, but they're just as lovely worn with today's full or straight skirts. Review the instructions beginning on page 14 and practice the point-de-Paris (pin stitch), decorative twin needle tucks, and the other heirloom techniques used here. Reproduction or other fine cotton lace may be substituted for the antique lace used in this project.

Materials Needed

Purchased pattern for a blouse with raglan or full set-in sleeves, opening in the back

Quantity of fabric called for in pattern

2-1/2 yards (2.3 m) lace insertion, 1 to 1-1/4 inches (25 to 32 mm) wide

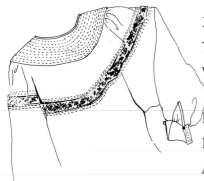

2 small pearl buttons

Twin needle

Wing needle (for point-de-Paris
  or pin stitch)

Hand sewing needle

Fine cotton thread #50 or #60

Appliqué scissors

Spray sizing

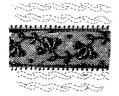

PROCEDURE

1. Prewash and press the fabric and lace. Place the pattern on the fabric on the straight of the grain and cut out. (There may be enough scraps left over for one or two collars.) Stay stitch 1/4 inch (3 mm) from the neckline's edge to prevent stretching.

2. Stitch the sleeve to the front and back seams using a French seam. Do not sew the side seams now. Place the blouse on a flat, well-padded surface and press with the seam toward the sleeves using spray sizing and a medium-heat iron.

3. Baste the lace insertion, starting at the center front and continuing over the sleeve seam to the center back. Set the sewing machine on a narrow zigzag and sew the lace to the fabric along the headers of both sides of the lace insertion. Trim away the fabric from underneath the lace, taking care not to cut the stitches or lace.

4. Set the sewing machine for a point-de-Paris or pin stitch and change the regular sewing needle to a wing needle. Point-de-Paris (pin stitch) along the lace insertion where it has been attached to the fabric. This step can be done by hand if your sewing machine does not have the pin stitch. (Practice first on a scrap of fabric.) Note: The pin stitch may be eliminated if desired.

5. Attach the twin needle to the sewing machine and stitch two rows of fancy or regular pin tucks on each side of the insertion. Sew more rows of pin tucks around the yoke or neckline, and on the cuffs. (Leave enough room for the seam allowance.) Place the blouse front face down on a well-padded surface. Spray with sizing and iron with a heat setting appropriate for the lace.

6. Stitch the side seams using French seams and press toward the back. Stitch the back seam, matching the lace and tucks at the center back. Leave an opening at the top. Attach the cuffs and yoke, and then finish the neckline and back opening. Make small buttonholes at the back edge or loops for small pearl buttons.

7. Finish a 3/8-inch (10 mm) hem at the lower edge by hand with an invisible stitch; or baste in place and then pin stitch with the wing needle by machine. Press. Hang on a padded hanger to protect the lace.

Antique Lace Clutch Bag

The perfect accessory for a summer dress or linen suit, a clutch bag is easy to make from an antique place mat, tray cloth, or hand towel. Although place mats usually come in sets of four, an odd one may sometimes be found in an antique or collectibles shop. Lace-trimmed hand towels are easier to find and more readily available. Searching for these unusual items is fun in itself, and occasionally a true treasure is discovered. The clutch bags can be made entirely by hand, or you may use a sewing machine for part of the project.

ANTIQUE LACE CLUTCH BAG

MATERIALS NEEDED

Antique place mat, tray cloth, or hand towel, approximately 12 x 18 inches (30 x 46 cm), washed and pressed

Fabric for lining, about the same size, washed and pressed

Pearl button

Hand sewing needle

Fine cotton thread #50 or #60

Spray sizing

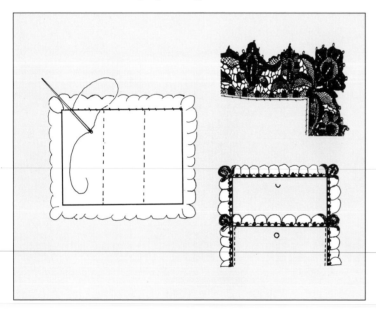

PROCEDURE

1. If working with a place mat or tray cloth with a lace border on four sides, measure the interior of the piece and add 1/2 inch (13 mm) to each measurement for a hem. Cut the lining according to the measurement. The lace border will remain unlined.

2. Press down a 1/4-inch (6 mm) hem on all sides of the lining. Attach the lining to the place mat or tray cloth with small, invisible hem stitches.

3. Fold the place mat or tray cloth into three sections and stitch the inside end to the back of the clutch bag at the sides where the lining is attached, leaving the lace border free. (See illustration.) Make a buttonhole or loop on the top flap and stitch the pearl button to the inside or lower flap. A covered snap closing may be used as an alternative.

4. If you're working with a linen hand towel with a lace border on one side, measure the fabric area of the towel and add 1/2 inch to the longest side for a hem. Place the right sides of the towel and lining together. Stitch by hand or machine along three sides of the towel and lining, leaving the lace edge open. Turn right sides out, and press with spray sizing.

5. Fold the lower section up and stitch along both sides with top stitching or with right sides together. Attach the lining to the towel at the lace edge with an invisible hem stitch. Make a buttonhole or loop on the top flap and stitch a pearl button to the inside or lower flap of the bag. A fancy metal or porcelain button may be used instead of a plain pearl button.

78

ANTIQUE LACE JABOT

Jabots are a delightful way to add a touch of lace to a tailored suit or jumper. Victorian women usually had several lacy jabots in their accessories' collections. Jabots can be made with purchased fabric and lace or from an antique item that has some damage. Since only a small amount of antique lace and fabric are needed, this project makes a wonderful way to begin working with the beautiful antique laces. Since jabots are an easy project for someone with heirloom sewing experience, you may want to make several jabots to add flexibility to your wardrobe and to have on hand as gifts.

Antique Lace Jabot

Materials Needed

9-1/2- x 9-1/2-inch (23 x 23 cm) square of fabric, fine cotton, silk batiste, or linen

1 yard (.9 m) lace edging, about 3/4 to 1-1/2 inches (20 to 38 mm) wide

1 yard narrow silk or satin ribbon

Hand sewing needle

Fine cotton thread #50 or #60

Appliqué scissors

Spray sizing

Washable marking pencil

Procedure

1. Prewash and press all fabric and lace to prevent shrinkage. Cut out the small square from the corner of the fabric. (See illustration.) Mark the lines for the bias French band with the washable pencil on a small square of fabric using a ruler. Straight stitch about 1/8 inch (3 mm) from the edge around all the jabot and the small square.

2. Trim the seam close to the line of straight stitches and then hand roll the edges of the jabot and the square. Hem the edges, or zigzag over the edge. Trim the threads. Press with spray sizing and a medium-temperature iron on a flat, well-padded surface.

3. Gather two rows of stitches on the inside of the jabot's neckline edge. Pin the edge of the lace to the outer edge of the jabot, mitering the corners. Ease the fullness and baste the gathered header of the lace to the fabric.

4. Set the sewing machine to a narrow zigzag stitch, and sew the lace to the fabric along the header of the lace. If the lace has edges on both sides, like the Alençon lace in the sample, stitch by hand to conceal the stitches along the cordonnet of the lace. A pin stitch by machine or hand is another way to attach the lace.

5. Place the collar face down on a well-padded surface. Spray with sizing and iron with a setting appropriate for the lace. Gather the neckline edge to a 4-inch (10 cm) length and attach a French band. Fold the ends under, but do not stitch. Finish the back of the neck by folding the French band under and stitching by hand. Thread a ribbon through the French band and tie it around the neck. Press face down as directed above.

Note: An antique handkerchief edged with lace can be substituted for the purchased fabric and lace. Cut a small corner as in the pattern above. If one of the handkerchief's corners is damaged, choose this area to cut the bias strip from. If the fabric and lace are in good condition, the cutaway corner may be used to make a second layer for the jabot. Follow the above instructions for assembly.

Antique Lace Wreath

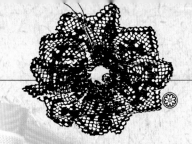

Materials Needed

14-inch (36 cm) grapevine wreath base

3 yards (2.7 m) lace insertion

2 yards (1.8 m) lace edging (different patterns can be used)

Dried blooms and foliage

1-1/2 yards (1.4 m) ribbon for a bow, 2 inches (5 cm) wide

Glue gun

Fabric glue

Needle and thread

Procedure

1. Spread a protective layer of newspaper over your work surface. Gently wrap the lace insertion around the wreath base, attaching it with fabric glue at the beginning and ending area where the bow will cover.

2. Gather the lace edging so the individual pieces are 10 inches (25 cm) long. Pull the threads tight and tie to form rosettes. Glue them to the front of the wreath at intervals with fabric glue. After the glue has dried, begin arranging the blooms and foliage on the lace edging clusters, leaving some of the grapevine to show. Secure the blooms and foliage in place with a glue gun.

3. Hot-glue additional blooms and foliage around the wreath. Do not attach blooms in the bow area. Fabric-glue the lace insertion along the center of the ribbon. Tie the ribbon in a bow and hot-glue in place.

Along with lace, Victorians loved flowers and were adept at drying and preserving them so they could be enjoyed year 'round. Young girls of this era often wore wreaths in their hair, and fruit and flower wreaths were often used as table decorations for special occasions. The flowers can be air- or silica-dried from your own garden, or purchased from a florist or craft supply store.

Victorian Lace Collar

1/3 yard (.3 m) fabric, Irish handkerchief linen or fine cotton batiste

3-1/2 yards (3.2 m) lace insertion, 1 inch (2-1/2 cm) wide

18-inch (46 cm) length of lace insertion, 1-1/4 inches (32 mm) wide

4-1/2 yards (4.1 m) lace edging, 3/4 to 1 inch (20 to 25 mm) wide

1-1/2 yards (1.4 m) entredeux

1 yard (.9 m) lace beading

1 yard narrow silk or satin ribbon

Fine cotton thread #50 or #60

Appliqué scissors

Spray sizing

Washable marking pencil

Procedure

1. Place the pattern on the fold of the fabric and cut out the collar. Mark the lines for the lace insertions with a washable pencil. Straight stitch about 1/8 inch (3 mm) from the edge all around the collar and follow the pencil lines for the lace insertion.

2. Machine roll the neck and collar edges. Trim the seam close to the line of stitches and then zigzag over the edge. Trim threads. Press with spray sizing and a medium-temperature iron on a flat, well-padded surface.

3. Gather the 1-inch-wide lace insertion by pulling the large thread or sewing a gathering thread in the lace header. Pin the ungathered lace edge to the

Victorian ladies often had several collars to be worn with each blouse, and their collars were often made with fabric and lace left over from a blouse. Then, as now, fine fabrics and laces were expensive, so nothing was ever wasted. Small projects like the collar shown here would sometimes be stitched when the ladies gathered for afternoon tea. This collar is the second of two designed to be worn with the antique lace blouse on page 75. Experience with heirloom sewing is needed to make this collar, so you should review the instructions beginning on page 14. If desired, reproduction lace may be substituted for the antique lace.

ANTIQUE LACE COLLAR (1)
CUT 1 OF FABRIC

LACE INSERTION

DECORATIVE STITCHING LINE

DECORATIVE STITCHING LINE

LACE INSERTION

LACE INSERTION

PLACE ON FOLD

ENLARGE TO 200%

PLACE ON FOLD

ANTIQUE LACE
COLLAR (2)
CUT 1 OF FABRIC

LACE INSERTION

LACE INSERTION

lower edge of the collar and around the shaped loop. Ease the fullness and baste the gathered header of the lace to the fabric. (The fabric will be cut away after the insertion has been machine stitched.)

4. Set the sewing machine to a narrow zigzag stitch and sew the lace to the fabric along the header of the lace insertions. Stitch the outside of the loop. Trim away the fabric from underneath the lace, taking care not to cut the stitches or lace.

5. Point-de-Paris (pin stitch) along the lace insertion where it has been attached to the fabric. This can be done by hand if your sewing machine does not have the pin stitch, or this step can be eliminated if desired. Place the collar face down on a well-padded surface. Spray with sizing and iron with a setting appropriate for the lace.

6. Attach a twin needle to the sewing machine and stitch a decorative or regular pin tuck about 1/4 inch from the insertion. Press down as directed in step 5.

7. Pin the lace beading to the neck edge. Stitch with a narrow zigzag to the neck edge, extending over the collar insertion. Attach a row of 1-1/4-inch insertion to the beading with the lace-to-lace method. Stitch another row of lace beading to the insertion to form the high neck.

8. Trim one side of the entredeux and clip the other side at 2-inch (5 cm) intervals. Extend the entredeux 1/2 inch beyond the top lace edge at the center back, surrounding the entire collar. Pin the entredeux across the lower edge of the insertion, extending 1/2 inch at the corner. Match the holes at the corners.

9. Replace the regular needle and adjust the stitch length so that the needle enters each hole once. Zigzag the entredeux to the outer edge of the lace insertion, starting at the opening. Trim the other side of the entredeux.

10. Gather the lace edging. With the right sides of the lace edging and insertion together, distribute the gathers evenly and baste to the insertion so that the heading of the lace edging meets the holes of the entredeux. Attach all around the collar and the top of the high neck lace band.

11. Turn over so the entredeux is on top, and zigzag the lace edging to the entredeux. This step may be done by hand with a whip stitch if desired. Gently pull the lace edging until it's flat. The holes of the entredeux should be open with zigzag or hand whip stitching attaching the lace.

12. Press carefully as directed above. Thread the ribbon through the beading and tie to close at the center back.

MODERN LACE CRAFTS

20TH-CENTURY LACE

Although 19th-century lace machines continually improved over the years, the major changes affecting the making of modern lace occurred with the development of synthetic thread fibers. These synthetic fibers produce fabrics that are used in every area of our lives, and even the space vehicles utilize these strong fibers. More than 60,000 fiber makers are employed in the United States alone to supply this 12-billion-dollar-a-year product made from oil and wood products that have been combined with natural gas, oxygen, nitrogen, hydrogen, carbon, and chemicals. When compared to the cost of natural fibers, synthetic fibers can be produced so inexpensively that synthetic-fiber laces have become accessible to virtually everyone.

The first man-made fiber was developed in France by Count Hilaire Chardonnet, whose object was to create an "artificial silk." He experimented with pulp extracted from mulberry trees during the 1880s, and by 1891 had succeeded in establishing a factory to produce the new fabric. Americans began to produce rayon in 1910, although it continued to be known as "artificial silk" until 1924. Chemically, rayon is cellulose derived from wood pulp, making it similar to cotton in that it originates from a plant. The name rayon comes from the surface sheen of the fiber "ray," combined with "on" to establish its link with cotton.

During the 1930s, large quantities of rayon lace were manufactured on the Leavers lace machine with antique patterns imitated from handmade bobbin lace. Today, rayon and natural-fiber rayon blends (cotton, silk,

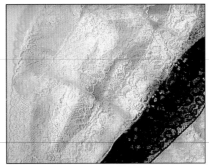

RAYON LINGERIE LACES FROM THE 1930s

and linen) have produced lace that is affordable by nearly every bride-to-be, and elaborate lace bridal gowns have enjoyed a surge in popularity.

Nylon, the first non-cellulose fiber, was introduced at the San Francisco World's Fair in 1939. Developed by the DuPont Company, nylon is a completely synthetic fiber made from petroleum that has been chemically combined with oxygen, water, and natural gas. Acrylic fibers made their appearance in 1948, while polyester, which was developed in England, became available in 1951.

Nylon and the other polymer fibers are exceptionally strong as well as lightweight. Nylon lace was used in the 1950s to lavishly trim evening gowns, when the designs had returned to 1850s styling, with full skirts over stiff petticoats and even hoops. Yards and yards of nylon lace were used for the ruffles of these gowns, which were also popular with younger women for their high school proms.

Microfibers were introduced in the 1980s. Finer than silk and usually made of polyester, they are often blended with other fibers. Much of the lace available today is made from polyester or polyester/cotton blends. Inexpensive when compared to the fine cotton laces of heirloom sewing, polyester lace is widely used for many of the lace craft projects included in this section. These laces wash well, and most need little or no ironing.

Leavers, schiffli, and other antique lace machines are still used to produce synthetic fiber laces. Improvements to the lace machines have been made in this century, although some of the technology has also been lost. (Some machines take as many as 20 years to learn the complicated steps involved in weaving airy lace networks.) Besides the leavers laces that feature a background net or mesh, there are many other styles to choose from. These include guipure, with its patterns connected by bars instead of net, broderie lace embroidered on white cotton, macramé lace, imitation Irish crochet, cluny, and tatting, as well as lace motifs that can be cut apart. Venice lace imitates the 17th-century needlepoint laces with sculptural scrollwork and floral patterns. All-over lace even comes in 45- and 60-inch (115 to 150 cm) widths, allowing full skirts to be cut with a limited number of pattern matches. A veritable feast for the lace crafter is readily available.

Among the lovely bridal laces are Alençon (featuring a raised cordonnet or heavy thread outlining the solid pattern areas), and Chantilly (featuring a silky thread outline surrounding deli-

cate floral motifs). Brussels lace, which has sprigs of appliquéd flowers on a net background, is another lovely lace available for modern weddings and other festive celebrations.

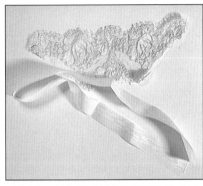
ALENÇON LACE WITH A SCALLOPED BORDER

Alençon is often used for the bodice of a wedding gown and as a border for the skirt. Chantilly lace, made in France today from rayon and cotton fibers, is one of the most beautiful laces available for special occasions. This silky, soft lace is lovely when gathered into a full skirt. French Chantilly laces are sometimes manufactured in 2- to 6-yard (1.8 to 5.4 m) lengths, imitating the patterns of the fine bobbin laces of the 17th and 18th centuries and the blonde laces worn by Queen Marie-Antoinette. While these laces are somewhat expensive, their cost would be many times more if made entirely of natural fibers.

Modern lace is worn in traditional and new ways, from evening dresses to women's neckties. In the 1990s, lace also decorates a wide range of casual wear, from T-shirts to blue jeans, as well as collars, blouses, vests, skirts, lingerie, stockings, hats, purses, jewelry, and gloves. As the 1890s Victorian style has recently regained popularity, our homes are again resplendent with lace and lace crafts.

BASIC INSTRUCTIONS FOR WORKING WITH MODERN LACE

Modern lace can be sewed and crafted with the same basic techniques and materials detailed in the first two chapters of this book. Following are additional tips and techniques for working with the projects in this section.

Allover Lace

These laces are handled like fabric and can be laid out on the cutting table over their lining fabric. The pattern is pinned to the lace and the lining at the same time, and they are cut together. Allover lace even comes in 45- and 60-inch widths, which allows full skirts to be cut with a limited number of pattern matches. The design of the lace should be matched in a manner similar to matching plaids by lining up the notches on the pattern pieces with the lace's design. The design at the front notch of the sleeves should match with the design at the bodice front armhole notch. The patterns at the side seam notches should also match. The front matches have priority over the back in case it is not possible to match the lace design at every notch.

Allover laces may have a plain straight edge or a scalloped border on one or both edges. The scalloped border usually serves as the hem and may also be used for the neck edge. No further finish is needed for the lace. The lining fabric may be hemmed to a slightly shorter length than the lace or zigzagged to the border of the lace with a narrow-width stitch.

The seams of the lace may be lapped, matching the lace pattern, and then basted and stitched along the outline of the lace design, first with a machine straight stitch and then overstitched with a narrow zigzag stitch. Any excess lace is then cut away from the seam. The seams are least visible with this method. The seams can also be stitched with right sides of the fabric together. The seam is trimmed to about 1/4 inch (6 mm) and finished with a zigzag stitch or other

seam finish. French seams may also be used to stitch the lace seams. The lining is stitched separately.

Flounce
A wide lace edging with a scalloped edge on one side or lower edge, and a straight edge on the other side or heading, flouncing is usually gathered into ruffles with one row of long, machine straight stitches.

FRENCH CHANTILLY LACE MADE FROM A RAYON AND COTTON BLEND

Galloon Lace
This lace features a scalloped border on both edges. It may be wide enough to use like all-over lace or so narrow that it needs to be used as a border. Alençon and Chantilly laces are frequently made in the galloon style.

Alençon Appliqué
This lace has individual medallions or motifs on a net background of Alençon lace. The motifs are first cut out with sharp scissors and then appliquéd by

hand with an overcast stitch along the cordonnet (heavy outline stitch) of the design. The stitches should blend in with the couched stitches of the cordonnet. The zigzag stitch on your sewing machine can also be used to attach Alençon motifs. Practice setting the width of the zigzag stitch until it just covers the cordonnet, and use an embroidery or satin stitch presser foot. Fabric glue does a nice job of attaching lace motifs as long as it is used sparingly and allowed enough time to dry.

Appliqué Lace Motifs
These motifs may be used as they are or cut apart (the edges don't ravel) and combined in your own designs. Cutting the connecting bars apart also allows you to shape the motifs onto uneven surfaces such as the picture hats on page 94. Remove or add bits and pieces of the lace motifs such as individual flowers and leaves to fill spaces and complete the design. Fabric glue is the best attachment method as long as it's used sparingly and allowed to completely dry, although the lace motifs can also be stitched to the surface just like the Alençon appliqués or stitched at intervals with a bar tack or several close satin stitches.

Appliqué Sleep Pillows

Known as sleep pillows in Victorian times, small pillows make a wonderful place to display the beauty of lace. Filled with fragrant herbs or potpourri, the pillows can be used to add fragrance and a touch of lace to bed and bathrooms. The smaller pillows can be hung from a bedpost or mirror, while the larger pillows can be displayed on a bed. For these pillows, individual motifs of Alençon lace were appliquéd by hand to fine net. The motif can be purchased separately at most fabric stores that carry bridal laces, allowing you the pleasure of working with a very special lace.

Materials Needed for Two Pillows

Alençon lace motif (one for small pillow; two or three of the larger size) or a lace appliqué motif (one or two, depending on the pillow's size)

1/2 yard (.5 m) silk, peau-de-soie, satin, taffeta, or linen

1/2 yard fine net or illusion veiling

2 yards (1.8 m) narrow cording

2 pieces of quilt batting

2-1/2 yards (2.3 m) narrow braid

Hand sewing needle

Thread to match lace and fabrics

Appliqué scissors and very sharp shears

Fabric glue, optional

Potpourri or dried fragrant herbs

Procedure

1. Create two patterns measuring 7 x 11-1/2 inches and 7 x 7 inches and place them on the fine net or veiling. Pin them in place and cut three of each pillow size. With the net still attached to the pattern, place it on the fabric. Cut one of each size for the pillow backs, and one of each size from the batting. From the remaining fabric, cut 1-inch (2-1/2 cm) strips on the bias or diagonal for the binding edge.

2. Trim the Alençon lace motifs with the appliqué scissors. The motifs may be used as purchased or cut apart and rearranged. (The heavy cord or cordonnet surrounding the lace indicates the top or right side.) Place the motifs on one piece of the net or veiling. Center appliqué designs look nice, but you can also place the largest motif toward one corner and arrange the remaining pieces of lace around it.

3. Baste the motifs in position and then whipstitch or overcast them to the net, following the cordonnet. The tiny hand stitches should be almost invisible. Appliqué lace motifs may be tacked to the net by machine, by hand, or glued in place with fabric glue.

4. Straight stitch about 1/4 inch (6 mm) from the edge of the remaining two pieces by machine, leaving about 3 inches (7 cm) along one edge. Turn right sides out to make a bag and fill with fragrant herbs or potpourri. Close the opening with an overcast stitch.

5. Stitch the bias strips together at their ends to form a 2-yard length and press the seams open. Fold the bias strip over the narrow cord and stitch with a cording foot attached to your sewing machine as close to the cord as possible. (A zipper foot may be substituted for the cording foot but it does not stitch as close to the cord.) Trim to 1/4 inch of the seam.

6. Pin the corded binding around the edge of each pillow, allowing 1/4 inch

for the seam. The finished edge of the corded binding should face the middle of the pillow back. Trim the narrow cord only, allowing a little extra fabric where the ends meet. Fold the extra fabric inside to neatly finish the continuous cord. Baste, then stitch. Clip the corners.

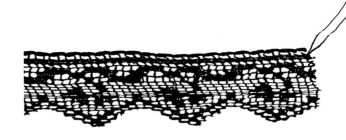

7. Place the right sides together so the finished corded binding and the lace are on the inside and baste about 1/4 inch from the edge, leaving a 4-inch (10 cm) opening on one side. Turn right sides out.

8. Insert the potpourri-filled net bags into the pillows directly behind the top lace-appliquéd net. The quilt batting should be beneath the pot-

pourri, next to the fabric backing. Overcast stitch the opening with tiny stitches to close.

9. Stitch the narrow braid around the edge of the pillows next to the cording for an attractive finish. Glue the ends of the braid where they meet. If you plan to hang the pillow from a bedpost or mirror, attach the braid with a bow.

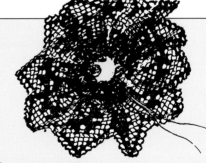

ℒACE ROSETTES

FOR THE PROJECTS ON PAGES 91 AND 93

MATERIALS NEEDED
FOR EACH ROSETTE

14-inch (36 cm) piece of lace edging, about 2 inches (5 cm) wide

Hand sewing needle

Spool of thread

Sharp scissors

Fabric glue or glue gun

PROCEDURE

1. Gather one edge of the lace edging on a sewing machine. Pull the thread to form a circle, matching the pattern of the lace. Tie the threads in a knot and trim the excess thread.

2. Glue the ends of the lace together at the pattern match. Use the rosettes to make button ornaments, decorate cones, balls, and other ornaments as well as a fireplace garland.

CHRISTMAS ORNAMENTS

Lacy Christmas ornaments are easy to make and add a light touch to holiday celebrations. England's Queen Victoria and her consort, Prince Albert (the German prince), made the custom of decorating an indoor Christmas tree popular, and this delightful German custom spread throughout the western world during the mid-19th century. The lace edging rosettes for these projects can be made ahead of time for a fun holiday craft party.

MATERIALS NEEDED FOR EACH BUTTON ORNAMENT

Lace rosette

Large, fancy buttons with a shank on the back

15-inch (38 cm) piece of gold cord or colored ribbon

2-inch (5 cm) square of fabric (metallics look nice)

Glue gun or fabric glue

PROCEDURE

1. Tie the gold cord or ribbon to the shank on the back of the button. Trace the button's shape onto the fabric square and cut out

2. Place a rosette behind the button with the cord behind the lace and glue in place. Glue the fabric shape onto the back of the lace to hold the cord in place and finish the ornament.

MATERIALS NEEDED FOR SIX CONES

1/3 yard (.3 m) gold metallic or other fabric

1/3 yard medium-weight iron-on interfacing

1/3 yard all-over pattern lace

2 yards (1.8 m) white lace flounce/edging, about 2-1/2 inches (6 cm) wide

1 yard (.9 m) narrow white lace edging

6 pieces of 20-inch (51 cm) ribbon or lace

Lace rosettes
(See page 89 for instructions.)

Assorted trims

Sharp scissors

Fabric glue or glue gun

PROCEDURE

1. Press the interfacing to the back of the fabric, taking care not to wrinkle the fabric. (Test a small corner first and adjust the iron's temperature if necessary.) Place the all-over lace on top of the fabric. Pin the pattern to the lace and fabric. Cut as one with sharp scissors.

2. Gather the lace edging and set it aside for trimming. Place a piece of aluminum foil on your working surface to protect it from glue spills. Glue the all-over lace to the fabric along the edges.

3. Form cones by placing glue on the back of one side and the front of the other side. Lap the sides about 2 inches at the top and just barely together at the

bottom. Set aside to dry thoroughly.

4. Make the ribbon or lace hangers by forming a 1-inch (2-1/2 cm) diameter loop in one end and glue. Fold over 6 inches (16 cm) at the other end, gluing about 4 inches (10 cm) and leaving a 2-inch loop at the top for hanging. Set aside to dry.

5. Glue the back of the cone at the seam (cover the cut edge) to the ribbon hanger with the point of the cone against the small loop of the hanger. Roll the small loop over the point of the cone and glue to cover the cone's cut end.

6. Decorate with narrow lace edging at the top of the cone and a rosette or wide-gathered lace edging or braid glued at the top edge. Glue the lace edging under or against the hanger ribbon at the back. Finish by adding assorted trims, and then fill with gifts or edible goodies and hang on your tree.

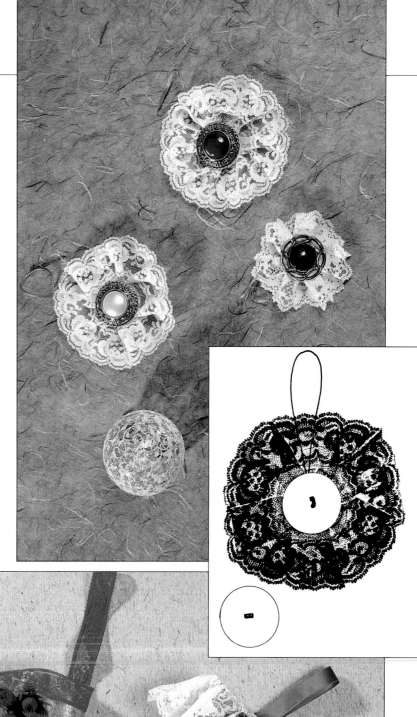

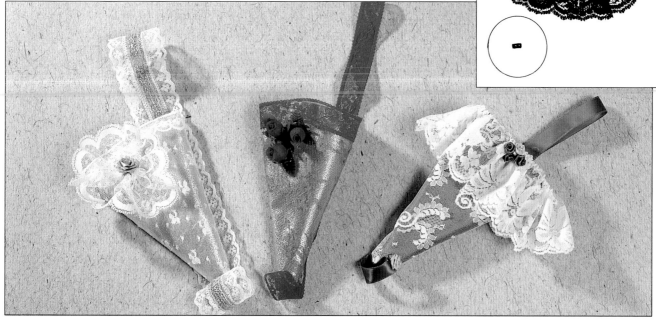

CHRISTMAS STOCKINGS ❀ ❀

Although Dutch children traditionally left their wooden shoes out on Christmas Eve to be filled with Christmas treats, it seems that the modern custom of Santa filling stockings appears to have originated with Clement Moore's 1823 poem, "The Night Before Christmas." These stockings are a fun, easy project, and help use up pieces of fabric and lace left over from larger projects.

HEM LINE

HEM LINE

LADIES LACE
CHRISTMAS STOCKING

CUT 2 OF LACE
CUT 2 OF FABRIC
CUT 2 OF INTERFACING

MATERIALS NEEDED

1/2 yard (.5 m) fabric, gold metallic, brocade, satin, or velvet

1 yard (.9 m) medium-weight, iron-on interfacing

ENLARGE TO 175%

1/2 yard all-over pattern lace

1 yard lace edging or braid, 2-1/2 to 4 inches (6 to 10 cm) wide

1/2 yard ribbon, braid, or lace (for handle)

Lace rosettes (See page 89 for instructions.)

Assorted holiday trims (roses, ribbons, bells, etc.)

Hand sewing needle

Thread to match fabric and trim

Sharp scissors

Fabric glue or glue gun

CHRISTMAS STOCKING

CUT 2 OF FABRIC
CUT 2 OF INTERFACING

STITCHING LINE

STITCHING LINE

PROCEDURE

1. Press the interfacing to the back of the fabric, taking care not to wrinkle the fabric. (Test a small corner first so you can adjust the iron's temperature if necessary.) Pin the all-over lace on top of the fabric, and pin the pattern to the lace and the fabric. Cut as one with sharp scissors. Remove the pattern and baste the fabrics of each front and back section.

2. Place the right sides together and pin the front seam. Machine stitch the front seam of the boot from the top to the toe and press. Gather a 2-inch-wide (5 cm) lace edging for the trim and set it aside.

3. Place a protective layer of aluminum foil over your work surface. Glue the all-over lace to the fabric along the top, bottom, and back edges, using fabric glue sparingly under the pattern areas.

4. Fold a piece of ribbon, braid, or lace for the handle in half. Glue it in place and set it aside to dry. Decorate the stocking with narrow lace edging or braid to define the stocking's style. Add a lace rosette or other trim if desired.

5. Sew the bottom and back seams of the stocking with right sides together. Turn right sides out. Press a 1-inch (2-1/2 cm) hem at the top opening of the stocking. Sew or glue in place. Attach the gathered lace edging or braid to the top of the stocking; glue or stitch it in place at the top edge.

6. Form the hanger by gluing a piece of ribbon, braid, or lace inside the stocking at the back, allowing about 3 inches (7 cm) of loop at the top. Add additional trims such as roses, ribbons, etc, if desired.

FUN ALTERNATIVE

Stitch some lace beading to an 18-inch (46 cm) length of 4- to 5-inch-wide (10 to 12 cm) lace edging or flounce about 1-1/4 inches (32 mm) from the top edge of the lace. Thread a 24-inch (60 cm) length of ribbon through the beading and gather it to produce a double-edged ruffle. Match the lace pattern, and glue in place. Pin the ruffle to the top of the stocking and tie the ribbon in a bow in the back.

WOMEN'S PICTURE HATS ❋

Women look wonderful in hats, and they seem to be increasing in popularity. Whether a gorgeous leghorn to complement a new spring outfit, or a more casual chapeau for a summer picnic, hats are fun and easy to decorate. The basic straw hats used in these projects range from inexpensive to moderate in price, and can be found in department and craft supply stores. Decorative hats for little girls and their dolls can be made with the same materials and techniques.

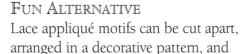

MATERIALS NEEDED

Straw hat

24-inch (60 cm) length of guipure lace (for the blue hat)

3/4 yard (.7 m) grosgrain ribbon for inside band, 5/8 inch (15 mm) wide

2 yards (1.8 m) grosgrain ribbon for bow and streamers, 1-1/4 inches (32 mm) wide

Fabric glue

Hand sewing needle and thread to match hat

Silk or dried flowers, optional

FUN ALTERNATIVE

Lace appliqué motifs can be cut apart, arranged in a decorative pattern, and glued in place.

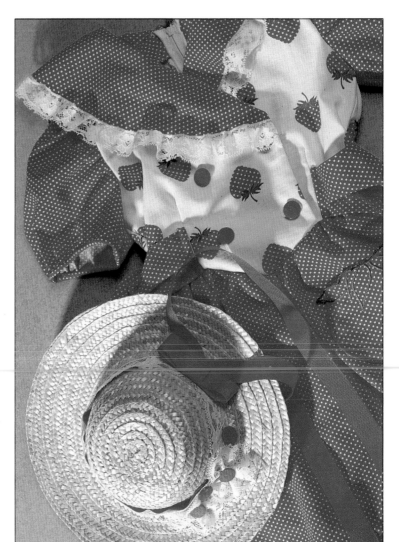

PROCEDURE

1. Machine or hand stitch the narrow strip of grosgrain ribbon to the inside of the hat. This helps the hat to fit securely and smoothly over hair.

2. Surround the brim with the guipure lace or the motifs and pin them in place. Fit the lace smoothly around the crown of the hat by cutting away some of the bars. Glue the lace in place with fabric glue.

3. Make a bow of grosgrain ribbon by folding the ends of an 8-inch (20 cm) strip to meet at the center point. Tack by hand. Next, fold a streamer over the center of the bow and attach it to the hat at the back.
   If desired, silk or dried flowers may be hot-glued to complement the lace's pattern.

LACE JACKET

An all-over lace jacket makes the perfect cover-up for evening dresses. The dress's color shows through the lace, accenting the designs of both garments. Double galloon (both edges scalloped) all-over lace was used in the jacket shown here. Although it tends to be more expensive than lace with a single scalloped edge, it saves time (no hems) and results in a beautiful accessory with the look of the Paris Couture.

MATERIALS NEEDED

Pattern for jacket

Quantity of all-over, double galloon lace called for in the pattern's instructions

Hand sewing needle and thread to match lace

Regular shears and appliqué scissors

9 clear nylon snap fasteners or small buttons

PROCEDURE

1. Press the lace face down on a padded surface with a steam iron to avoid shrinkage during future pressings. The iron's temperature should be set for the fiber content of the lace, and you should test the iron on a small swatch before ironing the entire piece. If your lace has a silk or rayon cordonnet (outline thread), set the iron's heat for it.

2. Review the directions for cutting all-over lace on page 86. Lay the pattern out on the right side of the lace (cordonnet side) so that the lower, finished edge of the bodice front and back hem is on the scalloped edge of the lace. Match the pattern at the center back opening and side seam line. The scallops should flow continuously all around the lower edge of the jacket. Note: If your pattern has straight side seams, pin them together before laying the pattern on the fabric and cut them as one. Position the sleeve pattern so that its hem is also on the scallop. The scallop may not match at the seam, but this seam won't be prominent.

3. Cut out the lace with sharp shears. An extra piece of 2-inch (5 cm) wide lace scallop edge was added to this jacket to finish the neckline. This piece will vary in length depending on your pattern's size and style.

4. Working on the right side of the lace, lap the side seams, matching the pattern as closely as possible. Baste. Straight stitch on the sewing machine along the line of the pattern match. Then set the machine on a narrow 1/16-inch (1.5 mm) zigzag stitch and sew over the previous straight stitch line. Carefully trim away the excess side seam allowance of lace on both the right and wrong sides.

5. Lap the shoulder and sleeve seams, repeating step 4. Try to match the lace as best you can, but remember that the line of zigzag stitches will create a pattern line by itself. Press face down on a padded surface, following the guidelines in step 1.

6. If the seam wants to pull away, zigzag stitch once more over the previous stitching. Baste the sleeves and high neck band to the bodice with right sides together. Straight stitch, then trim the seam to 1/8 inch (3 mm) and zigzag to finish the edge.

7. Finish the back opening with a narrow machine or hand hem. Attach clear nylon snaps or sew on small buttons and make button loops. A silk flower or a bow of complementary fabric can be added at the lower front of the jacket, although it's just as lovely without additional embellishment.

TUSSIE MUSSIES

*N*osegays of fragrant and symbolic flowers encircled by lace were carried by young ladies during Victorian times to dances, weddings, and other special occasions. Known as tussie mussies, these small bouquets were also used to decorate Christmas trees. Today, tussie mussies add a touch of Victorian charm to gift packages and other areas around the home. They take just a few minutes to make, requiring only light sewing and careful use of a glue gun.

MATERIALS NEEDED

15 to 25 stems of dried flowers, stems trimmed to 4 inches (10 cm)

28-inch (70 cm) length of lace flounce or edging, 4 to 5 inches (10 to 12 cm) wide

28-inch length of lace flounce or edging, 1-1/2 to 2 inches (4 to 5 cm) wide

28-inch length of lace beading

2 yards (1.8 m) narrow lace for bow

3 yards (2.7 m) narrow ribbon for bow

Thread

Glue gun

Green or white floral tape

CONTINUED ON PAGE 101

$\mathscr{S}$TOCKING BAG TRAVELING CASE ✸ ✸

$\mathscr{S}$mall fabric bags designed to hold personal articles (known as traveling cases) were almost a necessity for travel in the 19th century. There were many variations, but the most popular seems to have been a case that opened flat and rolled to close, holding many small items in various pockets. Because fine stockings were highly valued by Victorian women, a special case was often made just to hold and protect a pair or two of special hose.

CONTINUED ON PAGE 100

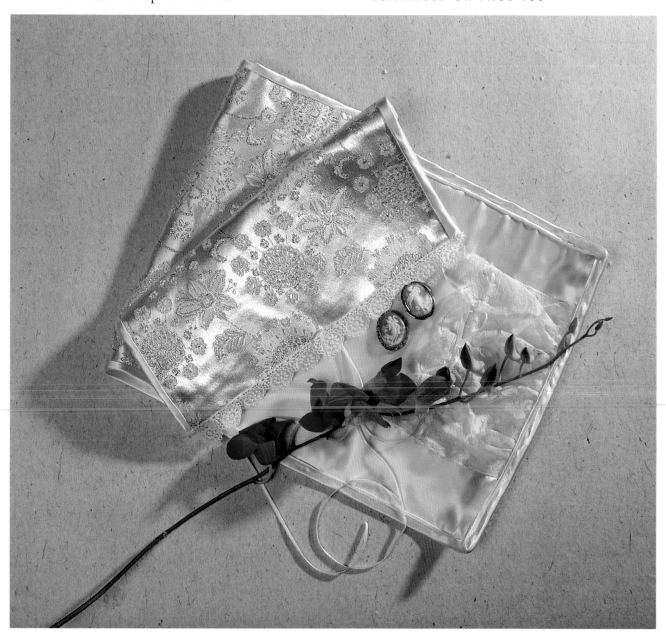

$\mathscr{S}$TOCKING BAG

Ladies' magazines like *Petersons* and *The Delineator* frequently offered patterns and examples of these traveling cases. The cases were made of fabrics such as linen, brocade, faille, taffeta, and satin, and were decorated with fine needlework and lace. This stocking bag was inspired by one that appeared in the February, 1884, issue of *Petersons Ladies' National Magazine*. The lace pocket inside adds almost no additional weight, yet provides a place to pack something special. All-over lace is used for this stocking bag, and is handled like one fabric along with the linings. A French band finishes the edges with a contrasting fabric.

MATERIALS NEEDED

  1/2 yard (.5 m) linen or brocade
   (for outer fabric)

  1/3 yard (.3 m) all-over pattern lace

  1 yard (.9 m) satin, taffeta, silk,
   or other fabric (for lining)

  1 yard medium-weight, iron-on
   interfacing

  2 yards (1.8 m) ribbon, braid,
   or lace (for ties)

  12 inches (30 cm) lace edging,
   5 inches (12 cm) wide

  12 inches lace beading

  12 inches lace edging (needed only
   if brocade is the outer fabric)

  Hand sewing needle

  Thread to match fabric and lace

  Sharp scissors

PROCEDURE

1. Prewash and press all materials to prevent shrinkage. (Do not wash brocade or satin unless they are made with polyester fibers.)

2. Place the all-over lace on top of four layers of fabric. Cut a rectangle measuring 11-1/2 x 30 inches (35 x 75 cm) of the lace and fabric and round the corners. (See illustration. You'll need four layers of lining fabric, or one layer of brocade and three of lining.) Cut a piece of lace from the remaining scalloped edge that's 5 inches wide or use lace edging. Cut four 1-inch-wide (2-1/2 cm) bias strips from the lining scraps.

3. Press the interfacing to the back of the outer fabric or lining, taking care not to wrinkle the fabric. (Test a small corner first and adjust the iron's temperature if necessary.) Place the right sides together of two pieces of lining and pin one end for a 1/2-inch (13 mm) seam. Repeat with the second pair, and machine stitch the seams. Turn right sides out and press. Baste the lace or brocade to one set of lining. Pin the pieces of bias binding together; then stitch and press the seams open.

4. Gather a 5-inch-wide piece of lace for the inside pocket at the lower edge. Attach a piece of lace beading about 1-1/4 inches (32 mm) from the edges of the lace pocket under 1/4 inch (6 mm) nd press. Stitch the pocket sides to the inside lower edge

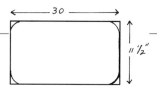

30

"½"

of the double lining, about 2-1/2 inches (6 cm) from each side. Pull the gathering stitches at the bottom and stitch to the lower edge of the lining. Tie a bow in the ribbon to take up the slack and make a pouch to hold something extra special.

5. Pin and baste the sides and end of both lining sets with the finished (seam) edges of both linings at the same end as the lace scallops. (The stockings are placed into the section formed by opening the two sets of linings.)

6. Pin one edge of the bias strip to the outside edge of the stocking bag, starting at the bottom. Match and stitch the seam in the binding to join. Trim the seam to a 1/4-inch width and press. Fold the other edge of the bias strip to the inside edge and hem by hand with invisible stitches or by machine with the stitch-in-the-ditch method.

7. Fold the piece of ribbon, braid, or lace for the handle in half and stitch. Roll up the stocking bag and tie with the ribbon wrapped around to secure.

PROCEDURE

1. Set your sewing machine on a narrow zigzag stitch and stitch the wide lace flounce to one edge of the right side of the lace beading. Stitch the narrow lace flounce to the other side of the lace beading. Match the lace pattern of the wide lace flounce and pin together. Cut 1 yard (.9 m) of ribbon and thread it through the lace beading. Make a bow with the remaining ribbon and the narrow lace.

2. Choose a special flower to be the center of the bouquet and then begin arranging the other flowers around it and hot-gluing them in place. A few stems of baby's breath sprinkled throughout the bouquet and around the edge is pretty. Continue gluing stems around the center flower until the diameter of the bouquet is about 4 inches.

3. Glue the lace together to match the ends of both lace flounce edgings. Pull both ends of the narrow ribbon to gather the beading and flounces, leaving only enough room in the center for the stems of the bouquet. Wrap the stems of the bouquet at an angle with floral tape, stretching it slightly as you work to release its adhesive. Place the bouquet in the center of the lace and hot-glue it in place. Glue the ribbon and lace bow to the stems and allow the streamers to hang down.

LACY HAND TOWELS

Lacy Hand Towels

Adding a little lace edging, insertion, or appliqué to a linen hand towel brings a special touch of elegance to your bathroom. In the Middle Ages, linen towels were embellished with lace-like drawn thread work and embroidery for church use. Lacy linens were in use by Italian nobility during the late 15th century, and soon after the custom spread throughout Europe and England. For these towels, appliqué trims or insertions can be cut from larger lace appliqués, or small medallions can be scattered on the front fold of the towels. Lace edging in a complementary design may also be added if desired.

Materials Needed
Linen hand towel (purchase ready made or make from a 12- x 20-inch, 30 x 50 cm, rectangle of linen fabric)

Lace insertion, edging, or appliqué

Blue or yellow washable pen (contrast with towel color)

2 spools thread to match lace and towel

Appliqué scissors

Procedure
1. Stitch a narrow rolled hem along both long sides and across one short side. Fold over 1/4-inch (6 mm) on the other short end and press. Fold again 1/2.to 1 inch (13 to 25 mm) for the finished hem. Stitch by hand or machine.

2. Pin the lace insertion, edging, or appliqué in place, measuring for evenness of the center and rows of trim. Allow 1/2 inch of lace to extend beyond the edge of the towel. Baste. Pin the appliqués in place.

3. Stitch in place with the sewing machine set for a narrow-width zigzag. Finish the edges of the lace insertion and edging by turning under and zigzagging along the edge. Carefully trim the excess lace with scissors. Place the towel face down on a well-padded surface and iron with spray sizing.

4. To make the white towel with white Irish lace and scalloped edgings, purchase a length of lace edging that's three times the width of the towel plus 6 inches (15 cm). Make the insertion by placing two rows of edging on the towel with the edges facing each other. (Make sure both pieces are right side up.) Machine zigzag the heading of one piece of edging in place, then baste and stitch the scalloped edge with a very narrow width stitch. Baste the other strip, alternating the pattern scallops to fit into the first lace edging. Zigzag the scallop first and then the heading.

5. To make the green towel with white lace, purchase a length of lace beading with edging attached that's two times the width of your towel plus 3 inches (7 cm). Baste; then zigzag the lace edging and beading above the towel's hem. Trim the edging from the remaining lace with a heading portion included. Baste the lace edging to the edge of the towel hem and zigzag.

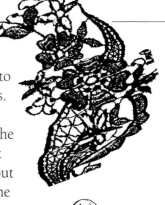

 LACE JEWELRY

For centuries jewelry has been made with ornamental openwork filigree interpretations of natural and architectural designs in metal, and ancient filigree-edged jewels may have inspired lace makers as they created similar patterns with thread and needles or bobbins. Today, there are many patterns of modern lace that resemble the filigree designs.

Basic sewing skills are needed to gather the lace; after that, all you need is a glue gun. Tweezers or small pliers may be helpful in making lace jewelry, and a warm-melt glue gun may be a safer choice than the traditional hot glue gun, since the work is very detailed. Findings for the earrings and brooches are available in most craft supply stores.

MATERIALS NEEDED

17-inch (43 cm) narrow guipure lace edging

Oval brooch finding with pin on back

Cameo medallion

2 earring findings (backs)

2 gold buttons, 5/8 to 3/4 inch (15 to 20 mm) in diameter

Hand needle and thread to match lace

Scissors

Glue gun or clear permanent glue

PROCEDURE

1. Cut three pieces of lace, one measuring 8 inches (20 cm) and two measuring 4-1/2 inches (11 cm). Gather the heading of the lace edging.

2. Match the pattern of the lace and the pin. Pull the gathering threads to form a flat circle and tie the threads. The center space should be about 1/2 inch (13 mm) in diameter for the earrings, and shaped to fit the back of the brooch finding, allowing about 1/8 inch (3 mm) for glue. Secure the edges with a small amount of glue and let dry.

3. Press with spray sizing face-down on a padded surface. Glue the lace edgings to the back of the brooch and the front of the earrings. Glue the cameo medallion in the center of the brooch finding and a button in the center of each earring. If you're using a glue gun, handle the jewelry carefully to avoid burns; if using clear glue, allow the jewelry to completely dry before handling the jewelry.

4. For the rose-centered jewelry, cut pieces of 1-inch-wide (2-1/2 cm) edging into 10-inch (25 cm) lengths. (If working with 2-inch-wide, 5 cm, edging, cut it into 14-inch, 36 cm, lengths.) Pull the threads tight at the center and tie to form a ruffled lace rosette. Glue the rosettes to the earrings and the brooch finding. Glue a silk or dried rosette in the center, and embellish with leaves, beads, or other objects if desired.

FUN ALTERNATIVES

Lace appliqués can be cut apart and the individual pieces of the design glued to the brooch and earring findings. A light coat of gold or silver metallic spray paint or enamel spray paint creates an entirely different look.

The Victorians were so enamored with lace that they decorated their homes with fanciful woodwork called Gingerbread. The eaves of gables and porches as well as balusters and columns were popular places for lacy scrollwork.

CONTINUED ON PAGE 108

LACE PICTURE FRAME MATS

Decorating picture frame mats with lace adds a special dimension to the images they enhance. Double mats create an illusion of greater depth and contrast, especially if the inside mat's color is darker than the outer one's. All over lace and lace appliqués were used for these projects, but any variety of lace will work. Keep in mind that the overall size of the mats must conform to the dimensions of the frame and the openings to the picture.

MATERIALS NEEDED

Pre-cut double mat board set (any shape will work)

All-over lace, about 2 inches (5 cm) larger than your frame's outer edges

Several pieces of appliqué lace

Fabric glue

CONTINUED ON PAGE 109

GINGERBREAD HOUSE MOTIFS

GINGERBREAD HOUSE GREEK REVIVAL HOUSE

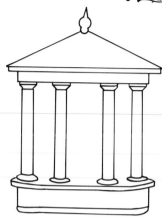

GINGERBREAD HOUSE GAZEBO

GINGERBREAD HOUSE TWIN GABLE HOUSE

ENLARGE TO 347%

GINGERBREAD HOUSE L-SHAPED HOUSE

GINGERBREAD HOUSE TRI GABLE HOUSE

MATERIALS NEEDED FOR EACH MOTIF

Cotton or linen clothing

1/4 yard (.2 m) all-over lace (one piece or scraps)

1 yard (.9 m) total scraps of lace edging and insertion

1 yard narrow ribbon, beading, or various trims

Water soluble stabilizer

Blue wash-away pen

Hand sewing needle and thread

Fabric glue

Several colors of thread

PROCEDURE

1. Prewash and dry the clothing, lace, and trims. Press if needed. Tape the stabilizer onto the pattern of your choice and trace the pattern onto the stabilizer with the blue pen.

2. For the gazebo, cut four 4-inch (10 cm) strips from lace insertion or beading. For the historic houses, lay out the background of walls on top of the stabilizer with all-over lace. Lightly glue the lace to the stabilizer with just a few dabs in the corner. (Too much glue will dissolve the stabilizer.) Straight stitch around the edge of the walls by hand or machine. Sew around the window and door openings.

3. Cut out the window area before basting the motif to the clothing. Zigzag around the sides of the house, the windows, and the door openings. The clothing's color will show through.

4. Make the roofs of all the buildings (except the three-gable Victorian) from strips of insertion or edging by layering them horizontally over the roof area. Stitch them in place. Define the vertical wall sides with narrow beading, entredeux, or a piece of lace cut out from wider insertion. Glue in place.

5. Edge the roof line and the gables with lace edging or trim. (Ruffles look nice.) Attach by hand or machine zigzagging. Next, define the porch railings and columns with lace. Make the shutters and window frames from narrow ribbon or lace trim, or leave them defined by the zigzag stitching. Glue all trim pieces in place.

6. Carefully tear away the stabilizer from the edges of the house or gazebo. (Any remaining stabilizer can be washed away.) Decorate the base and sides of each building with lace flowers, trees, or whatever your imagination creates, and glue or sew them to the shirt. *Note:* Hand washing is advised for the completed garment.

*L*ACE PICTURE FRAME MATS

PROCEDURE

1. Press the lace and allow it to cool. Spread a protective layer of waxed paper over your working surface.

2. If you're working with all-over lace, spread it right side down on the waxed paper. Place the mat with the largest opening right side down on the lace, and temporarily tape the lace to the back of the mat. Turn the lace-covered mat over to see if the design is straight and pleasing. Shift the lace and re-tape if desired.

3. Glue the lace to the back of the mat along the outside edge. Turn the frame over and cut out the picture opening with an extra 1/4 inch (6 mm) for turning. Carefully cut small slits in the lace, stopping just short of the mat's opening. Fold the lace around the edge and glue it to the back of the mat. (You may need to hold the lace in place with tape until the glue dries.) After the glue has dried, secure both mats together.

4. If you're working with appliqué lace, first glue the two mats together with the larger opening on top. Arrange the pieces of appliqué on top of the larger mat, and allow the pieces to spill over onto the inner mat's border. Starting in one corner, move the lace around, cut sections away, and add new ones until you find the overall design pleasing. Carefully glue the lace in place, taking care to only dab glue in thick areas so that glue spots won't show in the finished piece.

FRONT

BACK

CUTWORK LACE CRAFTS

THE TRANSITION FROM EMBROIDERY TO LACE MAKING

Cutwork is the link between the ancient needlework crafts of embroidery and drawn thread work and the making of needle-point lace. Modern cutwork, the English name for the lace that was first made by convent nuns in Europe, began sometime between the 12th and 15th centuries. A few of the monks may also have participated in the lace making, certainly to the extent of creating and drawing the cutwork designs and perhaps applying the needles themselves. Cutwork was used to embellish the priests' garments and the sacramental cloths that adorned the altars and accompanied Christian church rites.

Cutwork may have originated in the Greek or Ionian Isles of the Mediterranean Sea; however, several other countries in Europe also lay claim to being the first to make cutwork. The wealthy European port city of Venice, Italy, may have the strongest claim with its earliest version of cutwork. Known as "Punto Tagliato," this Italian or Venetian cutwork was made with a much finer linen thread than those used in Greek lace, and would later become the

prized Venetian point. Spain is another country claiming to have made the first cutwork. Cutwork was also made in France (known as "Pointe Coupe"), Germany (known as "Opus Seissum"), and in the Scandinavian countries of Northern Europe.

There were two types of early cutwork. The oldest variety was created on threads backed by linen, which produced a thick openwork lace, while the second, lighter version was embroidered on a framework of threads

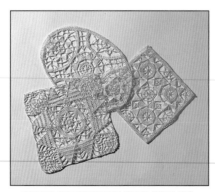

HANDMADE CUTWORK FROM THE 1500s

without a fabric foundation. The buttonhole stitch was utilized in both methods to make geometric patterns over the vertical and horizontal linen threads. Gold and silver threads, as well as colored silk, were sometimes used to enrich the cutwork lace.

The fabric and thread framework may have dictated the early geo-

metric designs of cutwork lace. Another design source may have been the architectural style of the early Gothic cathedrals, built first in France and dating from the mid-1100s.

The earliest cutwork of the convents began about this same time and could have inspired or at least influenced the cutwork lace made toward the end of the Middle Ages. The tall, ornately decorated spires of the church structures with their stained glass windows allowed light into the interior of the sanctuary, just as the areas cut away to produce the openwork of cutwork embroidery allowed light and space to become an integral part of the lace. In addition, many of the forms produced in architecture seem to have been reproduced in the lace.

Reticella was another early form of cutwork lace made in many parts of Italy. Its geometric patterns were mainly used for borders and designs on the interior sections of household linen and clothing fabrics. By the time of the Renaissance in the 15th century, cutwork was worn by the nobility to enhance the court costumes of both men and women, as well as the dignitaries of the church. Edgings were later added to the borders of cutwork to produce Point Gotico in Italy and Pointe Coupe in France. These intricate bordered cutwork laces were worn by royalty as well as the nobility throughout Europe and England during the 16th and 17th centuries. Lace collars and ruffs (fluted neck ruffles) and sleeve and boot ruffles decorated the ornate 16th-century costumes of the courtiers, who even embellished their boots and shoes with lace rosettes.

Cutwork had become the preferred needlework and principal pastime of the women of noble rank, especially those who had been educated by convent nuns. Queens, as well as their ladies and servants, passed long hours at court making cutwork for personal adornment and decorating bed linens with a profusion of intricate geometric patterns. Portraits of the late 15th and early 16th centuries show borders of cutwork edging the clothing, linens, and bed hangings of the nobility, and the robes and garments of church dignitaries.

Pattern books for lace making were available during the early part of the 16th century. Dating from 1527, one of the earliest was written by Metre P. Quinty and printed in Cologne, Italy, from wood block engravings. Lace designs or patterns were drawn directly onto wooden blocks or transferred to the blocks from parchment drawings. Ink could also be applied to finished lace, which would then be pressed onto wooden blocks to transfer the design. The blocks were then incised or engraved along the outlines of the geometric lace design. The pattern books were printed or stamped on parchment from the engraved and inked wood blocks. The patterns (usually white design lines on black backgrounds) were used directly from the books, explaining why the few surviving pattern books are in such well-used condition.

 When Catherine de Medicis (1519–1589), the daughter of prominent Italian merchant prince Lorenzo the Magnificent of Florence, married and became the consort of Henry II and ultimately the Queen of France, she brought the lace making skills of Italian noblewomen with her, and she's generally credited with establishing France's lace making tradition. Catherine used the Italian pattern books as well as her own skills to instruct the ladies of the French court, who spent much of their time making lace.

Samplers—known as samcloths—were made by young ladies of the courts as they learned the art of lace making. Containing many variations of the buttonhole stitch cutwork designs, the samcloths served as learning aids and future reference for a time when pattern books might not be available to the individual lace makers. Many of these samcloths were framed and exhibited rather than used in daily life, so they are in good condition and are featured in fine lace collections in museums such as London's Victoria and Albert Museum.

Designed especially for Catherine de Medicis and the ladies of the French court, the most famous pattern book was published in 1587 by a Venetian, Federic Vinciola. This pattern book was dedicated to the queen of Henry III, Louise de Vaudemont. The book exhibits patterns for Pointe

Coupe and contains many of the geometric cutwork lace designs that were available to the ladies of the courts of Europe. Vinciola's pattern book was reprinted for a number of subsequent editions from 1587 to 1623.

Another famous lace-making queen of the 16th century was Mary, Queen of Scots (1542–1587), who married Francis II of France in 1558. As a member of the French court and a skillful needlewoman, Mary learned many new lace making techniques from Catherine de Medicis. Returning to Scotland after the death of her husband in 1560, she brought her pleasure in

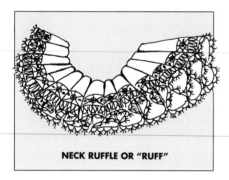

NECK RUFFLE OR "RUFF"

making lace with her. Later, in England, Mary consoled herself with the arts of needlework and lace making, even after her cousin, Queen Elizabeth I, imprisoned her.

Queen Elizabeth I, of England, adopted the French style for lace-edged neck ruffles and led the fad for the increasingly wider and more elaborate neck ruffles

"FALLING COLLAR"

popular during her reign. Starched and fluted, the ornate poinet gotico and pointe coupe neck ruffles assured that heads would be held high. Queen Elizabeth received many gifts of fans and other fine laces, which she enjoyed using and wearing throughout her long reign (1558–1603). Although she spent her time with affairs of state rather than in making lace, her support helped the lace making industry flourish in England.

By the end of the 16th century, the elaborately fluted ruffs had become flat collars made entirely of cutwork or of linen fabric edged with lace. The Puritan style collars, such as those worn by Charles I in the portraits painted by Van Eyck, fell over the shoulders and were worn by men all over Europe and England. Women of this period wore lace-edged Medici collars that raised up in the back and were brought into fashion by Marie de Medicis of France. The desire to wear and

use lace had spread to the people involved in commerce, as well as to the peasants, whose costumes revealed the lace making skills of the wearers. Lace was in great demand everywhere, even coming to America with the early colonists, who wore their Puritan collars plain for everyday but edged with cutwork lace on special occasions. A lace making industry developed that contributed greatly to the economies of the countries where it was made. Peddlers went from one house to another to show and sell the lace makers' art. European and English fairs gave the lace makers a chance to show their handiwork, while in Paris

*Lace Shop in the Galerie du Palais
J.E. Curiet
(after Abraham Bosse)*

the Passementiers controlled the commerce of lace ("passement dentelle").

During the 17th century, lace became more and more elaborate. Less and less fabric was

HANDMADE NEEDLEPOINT LACE, 1600s-1700s

used, until the fabric foundation was completely eliminated and replaced by parchment patterns that left the network of various types of buttonhole stitches (or "points") looking like they had been stitched in midair. Italian lace makers called their elaborate needlepoint lace *punta-de-aria*, or stitches in the air. The ladies of Venice produced Venetian point lace, a thick, intricate, almost sculptural lace. About the same time, point de France was made at the court of Louis the XIV, while in Spain, point de Espagne was created and worn by the Spanish Court. These elaborate needlepoint laces were often embellished with gold and silver threads as well as colored silks.

The designs of these beautiful needlepoint laces were most intri-

cate in the 17th century. They consisted of many variations of the buttonhole stitch (the basic stitch in making all needlepoint lace), as well as the wheels and rosettes which had been used earlier in the cutwork laces.

Toward the middle of the 17th century, European countries were producing many variations of needlepoint lace with a seemingly endless variety of stitches. Among the most beautiful laces ever produced, Alençon lace

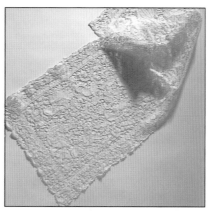

HANDMADE VENETIAN NEEDLEPOINT DRESSER SCARF FROM THE LATE 1800s

developed around 1665 from the earlier point de France. It was made during the reign of Louis XIV to satisfy the elaborate tastes of the French court and keep the money spent on laces imported from Italy and Flanders in France's economy. France's point d'Argentan and Italy's Rose or Venetian Gros Point and Burano Point were also elaborate laces made with a needle and a single thread.

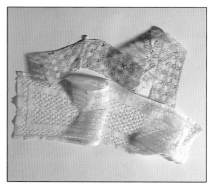

HANDMADE DRAWN THREAD WORK WITH CUTWORK ROSETTE STITCHES FROM THE EARLY 1800s

Fashion returned to more classical lines and less ornate styles toward the end of the 18th century, and the ornate needlepoint laces were too elaborate to complement the simpler, more classical styles. In addition, the needlepoint laces were so expensive and difficult to make that when the lower classes began to wear lace as an impor-

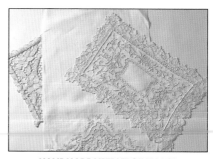

HANDMADE NEEDLEPOINT LACE FROM THE LATE 1800s

tant part of their clothing, the less expensive bobbin lace became fashionable. An interest in handmade cutwork laces was revived in the 19th century because the machines that produced much of the lace at this time were not able to reproduce the buttonhole stitch.

**ASSORTMENT OF HANDMADE CUTWORK,
1830s-1880s**

Proud of their needlework, Victorian ladies spent many hours using linen fabric and thread combined with the needlepoint lace stitches to

HANDMADE CUTWORK, C. LATE 1800s

produce a cutwork lace called Richelieu work or Richelieu guipure. Floral motifs and scrolls dominated the broad areas of

**HANDMADE CUTWORK AND LACIS SQUARES
TABLECLOTH, C. 1900.**

pattern, and were connected by bars which decorated many of the tablecloths, napkins, and other household linens of the Victorian age.

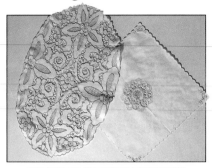

**HANDMADE CUTWORK DOILY WITH
NEEDLEPOINT FILLING STITCHES, C. 1880**

The pattern areas of Richelieu work were outlined with the buttonhole stitch (which was also worked over the bars), and picots were added to the bars during the progress of this work. When the work was completed, the spaces were carefully cut away, leaving an openwork effect. Usually for household linens, white, cream or ecru linen fabric was used with linen or cotton thread to match, although a darker shade of thread was sometimes chosen for contrast. Colored linen and silk thread was also employed, especially for more decorative projects and gifts such as needle or scissors cases.

During the late 19th century, a style of cutwork based on the patterns of early Greek lace emerged called Ruskin work. Named for John Ruskin, who thought that

the early cutwork patterns would look well on the handspun linen made in the English Lake District, the lace produced a cottage industry much like the early

**CUTWORK TABLECLOTH WITH
HANDMADE GREEK LACE, C. 1890**

Italian Reticella, and was worked in cut out square areas within the fabric. Tablecloths, napkins, towels, place mats, and tray cloths were made by the cottage workers who resurrected their spinning wheels to enjoy the process of producing the lovely table linens.

Victorian ladies also spent many hours making Ruskin work and other forms of cutwork by hand, utilizing the early stitches of Reticella and Greek lace. Pre-stamped linens were available along with matching thread from mail-order houses for those who lacked the skill or the inclination to design their own patterns. The lovely linens they made graced their homes, surrounding their families with the results of their handiwork.

During the 19th century, British missionaries to the Far East brought the skill of many forms of cutwork to the Chinese as a

HANDMADE CUTWORK WITH GREEK LACE FROM THE 1800S

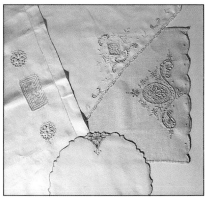

HANDMADE CUTWORK, DRAWN THREAD WORK, DOILY, AND CUTWORK LACE AND CROCHET INSERTION, C. 1900-1920

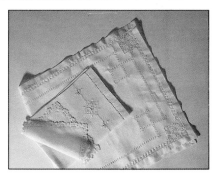

HANDMADE DRAWN THREAD WORK DRESSER SCARF, LEFT; HAND TOWEL WITH HARDANGER CUTWORK; BOBBIN LACE HANDKERCHIEF EDGING.

means of economic support. China maintains a flourishing lace making industry to this day, producing ornately decorated linens that they export all over the world.

Sewing machines introduced to the home sewer in the late 19th century were utilized for many modern stitching styles. Although they were intended to produce only a straight stitch, the creative Victorians expanded their limited capabilities. Many forms of cutwork and needlepoint lace were made by machine in addition to the work produced by hand at this time. Fabric with a design drawn or stamped on it was placed in a hoop. Then the feed dogs were lowered and the presser foot was removed, and the work was moved from side to side to produce the thin-to-thick lines of satin stitch outlines that delineated the pattern areas. Machine-stitched lace work remained popular well into the 1940s.

When the zigzag machines were developed in the mid-20th century, cutwork could be made on the sewing machine easily and quickly, while stitching along the pattern outlines with presser feet designed especially for making a satin stitch.

Today, as the art of making lace by hand is enjoying a new

revival, the stitches created in the 15th and 16th centuries are being used in new as well as old ways to embellish modern clothing and linens. Creative combinations of hand and machine made cutwork and needlepoint lace are prevalent in the fashions of the 1990s, while the pleasure of making fine cutwork is as great for the modern woman as it was long ago.

BASIC INSTRUCTIONS FOR BUTTONHOLE AND NEEDLEPOINT LACE STITCHES BY HAND

The Buttonhole Stitch

The buttonhole stitch is the basic cutwork stitch. It is used in various ways, sometimes in combination with other stitches, to produce many types of cutwork as well as needlepoint lace. There are numerous variations of the buttonhole stitch. Those presented here are the stitches needed for the projects in this book. Practice the stitches on a scrap of linen or other closely woven fabric before undertaking the projects.

The pattern is first drawn or stamped on firmly woven linen or cotton fabric. Then place the fabric in a hoop so that the fabric will be taut while the cutwork is in progress. If the fabric is very fragile, cover it with transparent stabilizer before placing the fabric in the hoop, or wrap the hoop with bias strips of a fine soft fabric such as silk or batiste. Tighten the hoop so that the fabric is firmly held in place. Choose a fine needle such as a sharp or between and a 20- to 24-inch (50 to 60 cm) length of

buttonhole stitches to follow. The stitches should be evenly spaced and equidistant from the edge.

Next, secure a new length of thread at the beginning of the row on the back side of the fabric with a knot or by taking several short stitches in one place. Insert the needle from back to front beneath the first row of reinforcing stitches. Point the

When all the design areas have been worked, the interior spaces are cut away. Sharp-pointed appliqué or embroidery scissors are needed to carefully cut away the spaces. Insert the point of the scissors from the back of the work and into an area in the center of the space to be cut out. Cut several slits from this center point to the corners and sides of

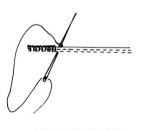   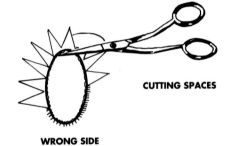

BUTTONHOLE STITCH   **CURVES**   **POINTS/CORNERS**   **RIGHT SIDE**   **WRONG SIDE**   **CUTTING SPACES**

cotton or silk embroidery thread knotted at the end. Threading several needles in advance will save time and help the work progress more smoothly.

Make two rows of short running stitches on the right side of the fabric along the pattern's design. The first row should be about 1/16 inch (1-1/2 mm) inside the edge, while the second row should be run closer to the edge of the design line, about 1/32 of an inch (.75 mm), and cross the connecting bars. These preliminary stitches reinforce the fabric and provide a guide line for the

needle toward the design line, and cross the thread under the needle at the edge of the line. Pull the needle through and repeat across the row. The corners are worked with the stitches to the edge worked the same length, while the lower part of the stitch is fanned out around the corner. For points, the inside stitches are made closer together. All stitches should face the space that will later be cut away.

The bars are usually worked before the main pattern areas. If picots are desired on the bars, they are made during the course of working the buttonhole stitch.

the space, creating flaps that may be rolled back to the edge of the line of buttonhole stitches and then carefully cut away.

Picot Loops
Picot loops are sometimes worked midway along the bars, especially in Richelieu work. They are very easy to make by stopping midway along the buttonhole stitches on the bar and wrapping the thread around the needle five times. Then insert the needle back into the fabric edge, make the next buttonhole stitch, and continue to the end of the bar.

116

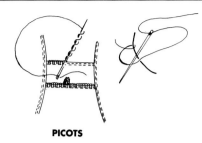

PICOTS

Filling Stitches for Hand-Worked Cutwork

Filling stitches are sometimes used in the spaces cut away from the main pattern design. These stitches form a delicate lace-like pattern when used with cutwork. There are many variations; those given here are used in the cutwork blouse project. The needle is threaded with a single strand of thread and inserted from the back of the fabric. Then the knotted thread is secured to a buttonhole stitch at the edge of the space to be worked. (Or you can take three tiny stitches to start the thread.)

Point de Bruxelles, Open Buttonhole Filling, One Stitch or Net Stitch

The easiest filling stitch consists of first making a loose buttonhole stitch in the first stitch of the edge row, then skipping the next two buttonhole stitches of the edge row, and making the second loose buttonhole stitch in the third stitch of the edge row. This process is repeated until you have worked around the entire space. The next row is created by making a loose but-

tonhole stitch in each loose buttonhole stitch of the previous row. As the space is filled, decrease the number of loose buttonhole stitches with each succeeding row. When you reach the center, pass the thread back down the line of stitches in one corner and secure it at the back of the fabric. The net stitch fills the open space with a taut, mesh-like lace. This stitch may also be worked in rows from one side of the space to the other.

NET STITCH

Point de Sorrento

The point de Sorrento consists of a series of stitches that are variations of the basic buttonhole stitch. Worked in neighboring areas or spaces of a pattern to vary the surface texture and design, they are an easy and interesting way to embellish needlepoint lace and cutwork.

Two Stitch

The two stitch is similar to the net stitch except that two buttonhole stitches are taken in each space instead of one. After a row of buttonhole stitches is worked across one end of the space to be filled, the two stitch is usually worked from side to side, reversing the work as you progress.

At the end of each row, take an extra stitch to secure the work into the buttonhole stitch at the side. Move up one buttonhole stitch along the space for each row. A row of net stitches is sometimes worked all around the space to be filled before proceeding with the two stitch.

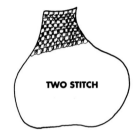

TWO STITCH

Three Stitch

The three stitch is worked the same as two stitch except that three buttonhole stitches are made in each loop or space.

THREE STITCH

One and Three Stitch

For this stitch, make three buttonhole stitches in each net stitch across the first row. In the second or reverse row make one buttonhole stitch in each space. Repeat alternating rows until the space is filled.

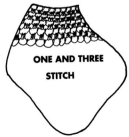

ONE AND THREE STITCH

Four Stitch

To create the four stitch, make two buttonhole stitches in each net stitch for the first row, and four buttonhole stitches in each space for the second or reverse row. Repeat alternating rows until the space is filled.

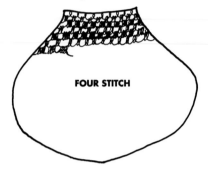

FOUR STITCH

Double Line Stitch

This filling stitch looks complicated but is actually quite easy. Work the stitch from side to side directly into a base row of buttonhole stitches at the edge of the space. A thread is passed from one side of the space to the other, and secured at the edge of the fabric. The second row is a row of net stitches that catches the first at 1/8- to 1/4-inch (3 to 6 mm) intervals. (The space of the intervals depends on the size of the area to be filled and the thickness of the thread.) Row three repeats row one; the fourth row has a tight buttonhole stitch that catches the center loop of row two's net stitch and row three's straight line thread. The steps are repeated until the space is filled.

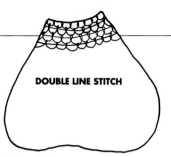

DOUBLE LINE STITCH

Twisted Bars

Twisted bars are used by themselves to fill an openwork area or as a base for rosettes. First secure the thread to one corner of the buttonholed edge, and then pass it across the space to the opposite corner. Next, take two stitches to secure and wrap the thread around the first line several times (the number of wraps depends on the size of the space to be filled) back to the point where you started. Secure the thread and pass the needle behind the row of buttonhole stitches to the second point. Take two stitches and repeat until a wheel is formed, with the spokes meeting in the center of the space. When the last spoke is wrapped, stop in the center and catch all of the spokes with two buttonhole stitches. (If a rosette is desired, take several buttonhole stitches in the center.) Then finish wrapping the last spoke with thread and secure the end at the edge of the fabric.

ROSETTES ON TWISTED BARS

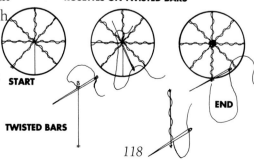

START

TWISTED BARS

END

Rosettes in Raised Point D'Angleterre

This stitch is worked in the center of the twisted bars described above. First attach the thread at the back of the work in the center of the wheel spokes. Working from the back, pass the needle under the first bar, then wind the thread back around the spoke of the wheel and pass the needle under the second spoke. Then wrap the thread around the second spoke or bar. Repeat until the round is complete. Six rounds are usually needed for a complete rosette, although more may be needed if the space is large. The right side should have a raised or corded effect over each spoke of the wheel.

ROSETTES - RAISED POINT D'ANGLETERRE

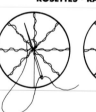

MACHINE CUTWORK

Cutwork is easy to make on your sewing machine. Follow the same steps for transferring the design to the fabric as for hand work. The design may be traced onto a piece of transparent, water-dissolving stabilizer which is then basted to the fabric. There is less restriction in the fabric base when working by machine, so the fabric base may be firmly woven linen or cotton or a synthetic. The pillowcase project in this section is made on a cotton polyester batiste fabric, which is suitable for machine cutwork but not for work done by hand. While they are not necessary with hand cutwork, interfacing or stabilizer are absolutely necessary when working by machine.

The work may be stitched flat or placed in a hoop. If a hoop is used, lower or cover the feed dogs of the sewing machine before stitching. The presser foot is removed, and the work is then moved along the pattern lines in a freehand motion. Various widths of zigzag stitches may be used with this freehand technique. For very fine fabrics, wrap the hoop with fabric strips before placing the fabric in the hoop. Tighten the hoop before starting to sew.

Begin the cutwork by machine stitching with a regular straight stitch along the entire line of the design. A single row of machine reinforcing stitches is usually sufficient, since the width of the satin stitch is controlled by the machine instead of the individual, although two rows of reinforcing stitches may be needed if the fabric is loosely woven or very fine. Start at the center of the motif and work toward the edges. Fill the petal edges of the roses (that will later have a wide zigzag stitch) with reinforcing stitches so they will have a padded effect.

Zigzag with the sewing machine set for a 1/8-inch width. Start with the connecting bars, then do the outer rims or edges, and then do the leaves and buds. The roses are the last part of the design to be worked. They may be stitched with varying widths of zigzag stitch, starting with the narrow areas and gradually widening the stitch for the petal edges. This takes some practice, so it's advisable to use a scrap of fabric and practice until you are comfortable with adjusting stitch widths while working.

The next step is to cut out the areas or spaces marked with an X, being very careful not to cut the threads. Use sharp-pointed scissors like appliqué or embroidery scissors. Insert the point of the scissors into the center areas, and then cut toward each corner, stopping just short of the stitches. Working from the wrong side of the fabric, fold the fabric back and carefully trim along the line of stitches. If a stitch is cut by mistake, a tiny dab of fabric glue can save the project.

Remove the work from the hoop, and then remove the stabilizer by tearing or trimming it away from the line of stitches or dissolve the stabilizer by running it under cold water. The water should also remove any leftover traces of the marker. Place the article face down on a well-padded surface, and iron from the back with a little spray sizing. The stitches should be raised up slightly above the fabric.

To add lace or net as a ground for the cut out areas of the design, baste the lace or net to the back of the fabric before straight stitching the outline of the design. Proceed as directed above until all areas of the motif have been completed. Working on the right side of the garment, cut only the fabric and interfacing of the lace or net ground area, working one layer at a time and being very careful not to pierce through the lace. The lace or net should remain to fill the space where the fabric is cut away. Trim any excess lace or net from the back of the work.

CUTWORK ROSES DRESS ❊ ❊ ❊

*M*odern machine-stitched cutwork roses surround the neckline of this dress using lace in the cutout spaces to imitate the needlepoint stitches so popular in the 19th century. Today's modern sewing machines allow us to make this 20th century interpretation of cutwork by using the zigzag or satin stitch and pieces of lace with a decorative ground. Roses were a favorite design of Victorian ladies. The cutwork may also be worked by hand using the ancient buttonhole stitch.

MATERIALS NEEDED

Dress with plain neckline

1 yard (.9 m) lace with a simple pattern background or net or tulle

Water-soluble stabilizer

Blue or yellow wash-away pen

Sulky rayon thread (for machine work) or embroidery cotton and needle (for hand work)

Appliqué scissors or embroidery scissors

8- or 10-inch (20 or 25 cm) embroidery hoop

PROCEDURE

1. Trace the rose motif onto the stabilizer with the wash-away pen. Line up the dress' shoulder seams and baste the stabilizer to the neckline. Baste the lace ground over the rose motifs at the back of the work.

2. Straight stitch by machine along the entire design line, starting at the center of the rose and working outward to reinforce and pad the stitches. Fill in the petal edge areas of the roses that are to be stitched with a wide zigzag. If working by hand, use the running stitch and a double row of stitches.

3. Zigzag with the sewing machine set for a stitch about 1/8 inch (3 mm) wide. Start with the leaves and buds. If doing the work by hand, use a buttonhole stitch for these areas.

4. The roses may be stitched with varying widths of zigzag stitches. (Practice on another piece of fabric before doing this step.) A satin stitch is used here when working by hand.

5. Cut out the fabric only from areas marked with an X, being very careful not to cut the zigzag threads or lace. Insert the point of the scissors into the center of the area to be cut out. Cut to each corner, then trim.

6. Remove the stabilizer from the neckline by trimming or tearing around the outer edge of the design, or dissolve by running the dress under cold water. The water should also remove any remaining traces of the marker.

7. Press face down on a terry towel or padded base from the back using spray sizing.

DRESS CUTWORK PATTERN

INCREASE TO FIT NECKLINE

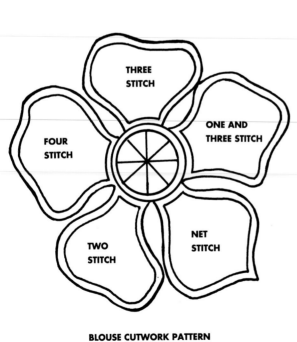

THREE STITCH

ONE AND THREE STITCH

FOUR STITCH

NET STITCH

TWO STITCH

BLOUSE CUTWORK PATTERN

**CENTER ROSETTE RAISED
POINT D'ANGLETERRE**

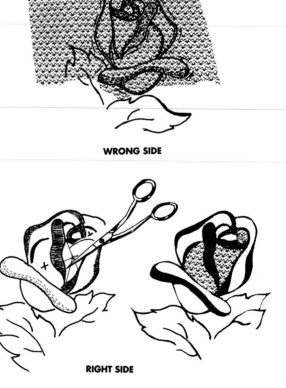

WRONG SIDE

RIGHT SIDE

CUTWORK NEEDLEPOINT LACE BLOUSE ❀❀

The last rose of the season unfolded its creamy petals to reveal a golden sunburst at the center. Each petal was unique from its neighbor, and inspired the cutwork rose motif for this blouse. Each petal is interpreted in a different needlepoint lace stitch, much as the 17th and 18th century lace makers would have worked their exquisite floral point laces. The center rosette is raised point d'Angleterre, while the petals are stitched in point de Bruxelles and variations of point de Sorrento. This is an intermediate level project to be worked by hand using the ancient buttonhole stitch.

❦

MATERIALS NEEDED

Linen blouse

Blue or yellow wash-away pen

Embroidery cotton DMC or equal thread

Appliqué scissors

6-inch (15 cm) embroidery hoop

❦

PROCEDURE

1. Trace the rose motif onto the center front of the blouse with the wash-away pen. Place the blouse in the hoop to hold the fabric taut.

2. Straight stitch by machine along the entire design line, starting at the center of the rose and working out-ward to reinforce the edges and pad the buttonhole stitches. If working by hand, use two rows of short running stitches.

3. Working on the right side of the fabric, buttonhole stitch around the center wheel and each petal. Cut out the areas marked with an X, being very careful not to cut the buttonhole stitch threads. Insert the point of the scissors into the center of the area to be cut out. Cut to each corner, then fold the fabric to the back and trim from the wrong side of the work.

4. Fill the petal areas with the needle-point stitches indicated in the diagram. See pages 116-119 for detailed instructions.

5. Remove the blouse from the hoop. Press, face down on a terry towel or padded surface from the back using spray sizing.

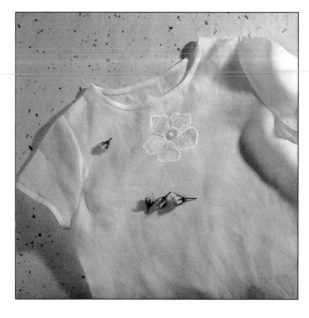

CUTWORK LACE BLOUSE

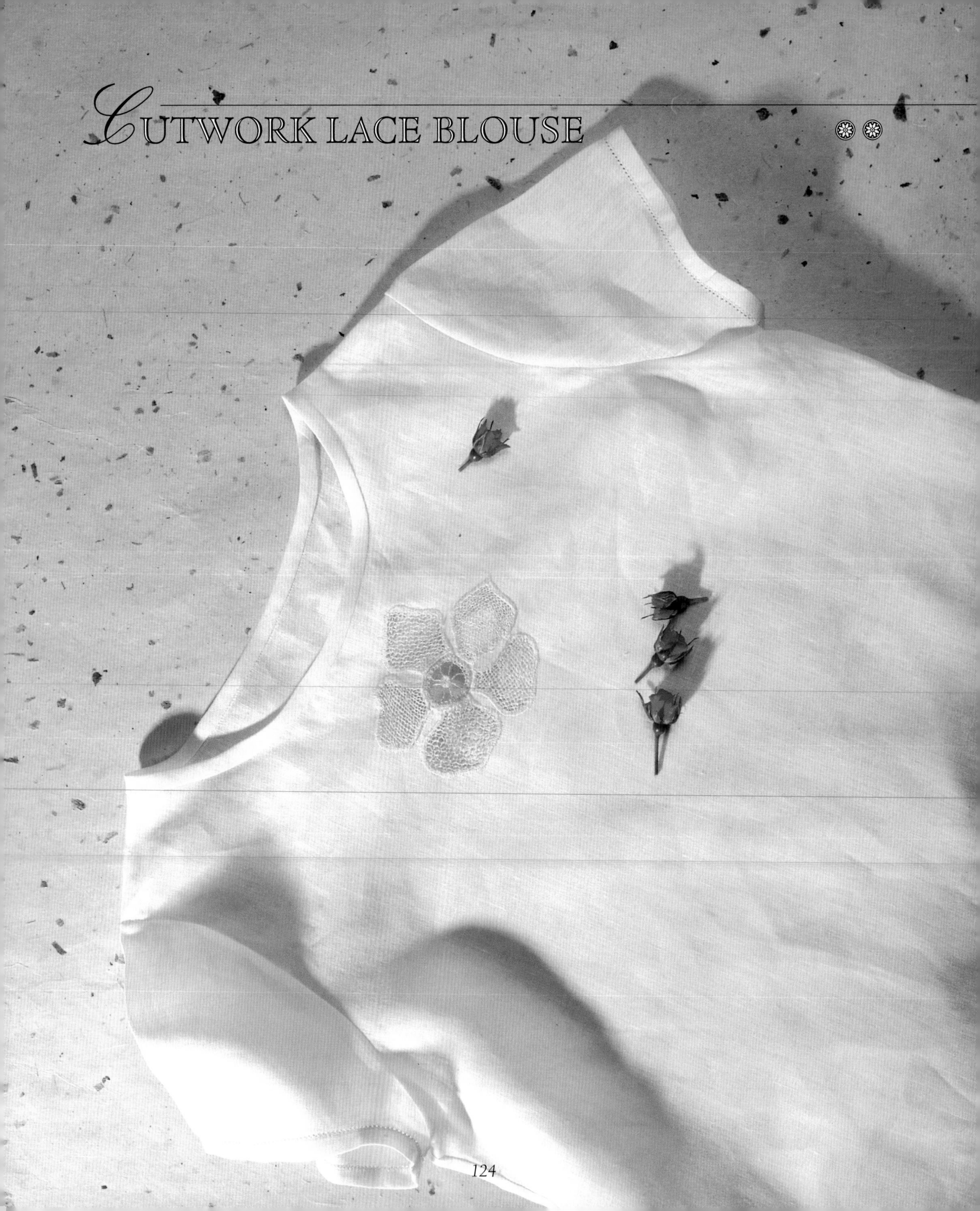

CUTWORK ROSES PILLOW CASE

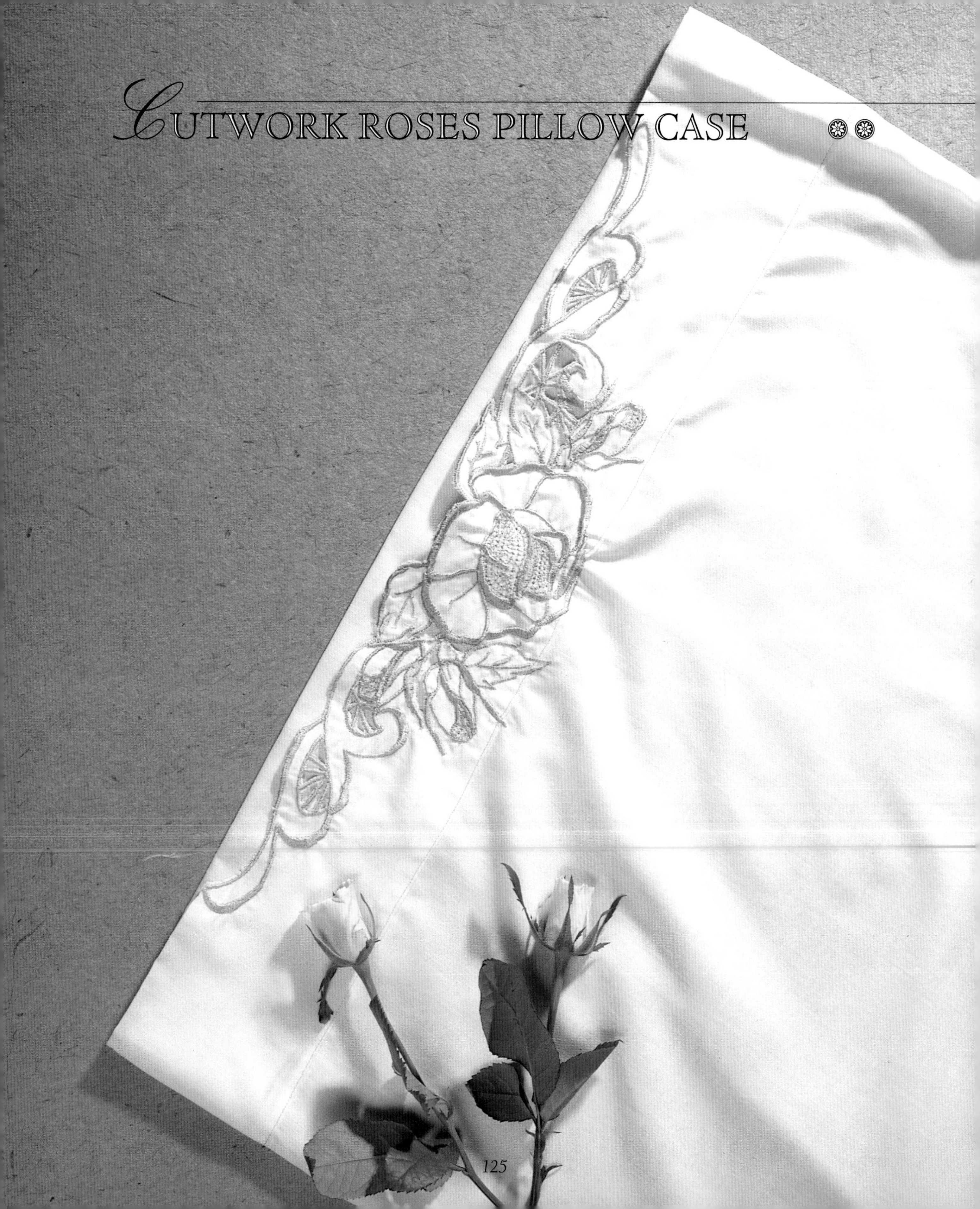

CUTWORK ROSES PILLOW CASE

Cutwork, the preferred handwork of the 16th-century Queen Catherine de Medici, was stitched by ladies of high birth in their castles and was the favorite court pastime. The openwork embellishment was used to decorate their bed linens as well as clothing, and colored silk threads often brightened the design.

Although many variations of cutwork were traditionally made by hand with a needle, modern sewing machines allow us to make an interpretation of cutwork by using the zigzag or satin stitch and the pin stitch. Please refer to the basic buttonhole stitch instructions on page 27 and to page 26 for the pin stitch fillings instructions.

MATERIALS NEEDED

Purchased linen pillow case

Water-soluble stabilizer

Blue or yellow wash-away pen

Thread to match fabric

3 colors of bulky rayon thread (if working by machine) or cotton (handwork)

Appliqué scissors

8- or 10-inch (20 to 25 cm) embroidery hoop

PROCEDURE

1. Trace the rose motif onto the stabilizer with the wash-away pen. Center

the stabilizer on the front side of the pillow case and pin or baste in place.

2. If the cutwork is to be done by hand, place the stabilizer and pillow case in the hoop. Turn the pillow case inside out.

3. If working by machine, straight stitch along the entire design line, starting at the center of the rose and working outward. (This will reinforce and pad the stitches.) Fill in the petal edge areas of the roses with a wide zigzag. If working by hand, use the running stitch and a double row of stitches.

4. Cut one layer of the fabric away in the areas indicated by dots and fill with the pin stitch. (See pages 116-119 for basic instructions.)

5. Zigzag with the sewing machine set for a stitch about 1/8-inch (3 mm) wide.

Start with connecting bars, then work the scrolls, and then the leaves and buds. If doing the work by hand, use a buttonhole stitch for these areas.

6. The roses can be stitched with varying widths of zigzag stitch. (Practice on another piece of fabric before doing this step.) Use a satin stitch for this step when working by hand.

7. Cut out the areas marked with an X, being very careful not to cut the zigzag threads. Insert the point of the scissors into the center of the area to be cut out. Cut to each corner, then trim.

8. Remove the pillow case from the hoop. Remove the stabilizer from the case by trimming or tearing around the outer edge of the design, or dissolve it by running the pillow case under cold water. The water should also remove any remaining trace of the marker.

9. Press face down on a terry towel or padded surface and iron from the back with spray sizing.

ACTUAL SIZE

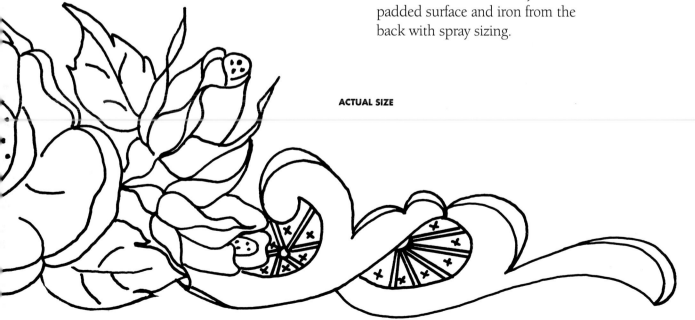

: : : **PIN STITCH INSERTION**

ROSE MOTIF HAND TOWEL

Cutwork is the modern version of Reticella lace, a needle lace made first in Italy during the 15th century and much prized by European royalty. Portraits show that it was worn by the Elizabethans as neckruffs and cuffs, and was an important part of their elaborate court costumes.

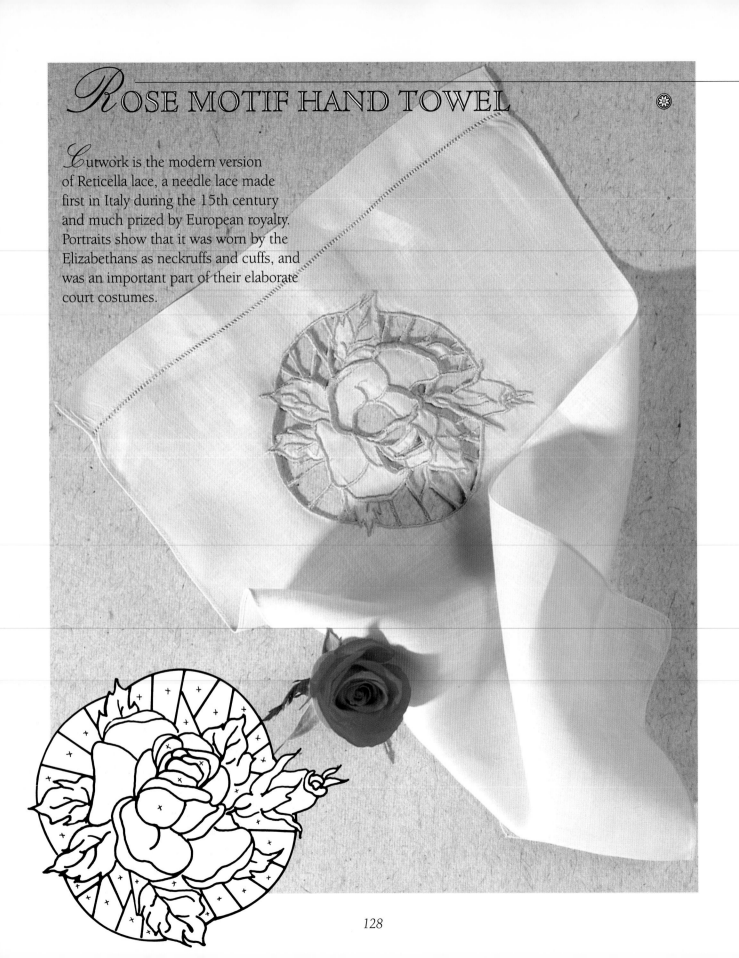

MATERIALS NEEDED

Linen hand towel (purchased ready made or made with a 12- x 20-inch, 30 x 50 cm, rectangle of linen fabric)

Water soluble stabilizer or light, tear-away fabric

Blue or yellow washable pen

Embroidery cotton or rayon thread

Hand embroidery needle (needed only if doing work by hand instead of machine)

Appliqué scissors

8- or 10-inch (20 or 25 cm) embroidery hoop

Spray sizing

PROCEDURE

1. Stitch a narrow rolled hem along both long sides and across one of the short ends. Fold over 1/4 inch (6 mm) on the other short end and press. Fold again 1-inch-wide (2-1/2 cm) for a finished hem and machine or hand stitch. (Skip this step if your towel is ready made.)

2. Trace the rose motif onto the center front of the towel with the washable pen. Pin or baste a piece of stabilizer to the back of the towel and place it in the hoop. Remove foot and cover or lower feed dogs on your sewing machine. (It may be necessary to remove the needle in order to slip the towel and hoop into a stitching position.)

3. Machine stitch with regular straight stitch along the entire line of the design, starting at the center of the rose and working outward to reinforce and pad the stitches. Fill in the areas of the center rose that are to be stitched with a wide zigzag.

4. Zigzag with the sewing machine set for a stitch about 1/8 inch (3 mm) wide, starting with the connecting bars, then the outer rim, and then the leaves and bud. If working by hand, use a buttonhole stitch for these areas.

5. Stitch the center rose with varying widths of zigzag stitches. (Practice on another piece of fabric before doing this step.) If working by hand, use a satin stitch for this step.

6. Cut out the areas marked with an X, taking care not to cut the zigzag threads. Insert the point of the scissors into the center of the area to be cut out. Cut to each corner, then trim.

7. Remove the towel from the hoop. Next, remove the stabilizer from the towel by trimming or tear out around the outer edge of the design. If necessary, you can dissolve the stabilizer by running the towel under cold water. (The water will also remove any remaining trace of the marker.)

8. Place the towel face down on a terry towel or padded base, and iron from the back with spray sizing. If desired, lace may be added to the wide hem edge.

BATTENBERG LACE CRAFTS

Battenberg lace is one of the "modern lace" styles of lace crafts that became popular with Victorian ladies during the 19th century. Lace tapes (or braids) are connected with filling stitches worked with a needle and a single thread to define a pattern. The tape laces were created for those who simply enjoyed the art of lace making in their spare time, rather than for professional lace makers. Battenberg lace represents the combination of the bobbin laces (tape) and needlepoint laces (filling stitches) made by skilled lace makers in the 15th–18th centuries.

Bobbin lace was the precursor of the 19th century tape laces. During the 16th century, it was made in Europe, especially in Flanders, an area that contained the present-day city of Brussels. There were several ways to make the flowing designs of the early bobbin laces, which were made on a pillow with many pairs of bobbins or spindles wound with fine linen thread.

Skilled lace makers could work the background and design for a whole width of lace as one piece. Intricate designs often took hundreds of bobbins and many hours of work to complete a short length.

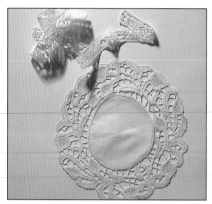

HANDMADE BOBBIN LACE (TAPE LACE INSERTION) AND HANDMADE MILANESE BOBBIN LACE DOILY, C. 1850

The braid could also be made separately with the connecting background added later. This method influenced the designs and techniques of the 19th century modern laces. The narrow

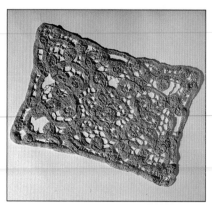

HANDMADE BOBBIN TAPE LACES, C. 1860

braid or tape was worked in a long, straight strip, and this was usually a beginner's first bobbin lace because it required fewer bobbins and a simpler pattern with frequent repeats. Most of the lace makers were women; however, both girls and boys were

taught to make bobbin lace at a very early age. Men would sometimes sit down to a pillow in the evening, after completing their regular day's work. Sometimes the tape or braid was attached to a net or meshlike background worked as a separate strip of bobbin lace. The narrow tapes or braid were also laid out on a fabric or parchment pattern. Where the tapes rounded the corners, two or three gathering stitches were taken to remove the slack. Then the needlepoint background stitches could be worked, usually by more experienced lace makers.

The needlepoint stitches filling the spaces of 19th-century tape laces were made with a needle and a single strand of thread, similar to the cutwork and needlepoint laces of the Renaissance. Originating with ancient cutwork and the basic buttonhole stitch, the filling stitches evolved from the 14th and 15th century development of Greek lace and Italy's Reticella lace.

Cutwork was the main pastime of nuns and ladies of noble birth. Lace makers in European countries, especially Italy, Spain, and France, as well as Flanders, created many variations of the basic buttonhole stitch to produce the elegant needlepoint laces of the

17th and 18th centuries. Many of these needlepoint or "point" lace stitches were adapted for use with tapes or braids for the modern lace of the 19th century.

Lace making was also a favorite pastime for ladies during the 1840s and 1850s. Many hours were pleasantly devoted to the

HANDMADE RENAISSANCE TAPE LACE COLLAR FROM THE 1860S

fine craft of making "real" lace, which was worked entirely by hand. (Since lace making was just a hobby for most Victorian ladies, rather than a profession, their laces were usually limited in complexity. Some of the ladies, though, were able to produce excellent braids or tapes, which were then combined with the needlepoint stitches used to make modern point lace that looked very intricate.

An alternative to handmade tapes and braids were those made by a French circular braiding machine called the Barmen. Originally

designed to make a diagonal weave braid, the Barmen manu-

MACHINE-MADE BATTENBERG LACE TAPES AND HANDMADE NEEDLEPOINT STITCHES, C. 1895.

factured many varieties of tapes or braids which were often used by the ladies to make the work go faster. The completed modern lace was called "imitation" lace. Less time-consuming and easier to make, the "imitation" tape or point laces were used for large table and bed coverings, parasols and jackets, as well as collars, fans, baby bonnets, and other small projects.

There were many different varieties and styles of tape available, so modern point lace evolved with many different names utilizing different tapes and stitches. Magazines, known then as periodicals and journals, were very popular with Victorian ladies. Those published from the 1830s through the 19th and early 20th centuries regularly included patterns for various kinds of point

lace with instructions for a large variety of needlepoint filling stitches. The August 1857 edition of *Godey's Lady's Book* included a pattern for a "Point Lace Infant's Cap" made from "very fine Parisian cotton braid."

Other varieties of cotton and linen tapes and braids available in the middle of the 19th century included Bruges braids, Duchesse braids, Renaissance braids, Honiton braids and insertions for Princess Lace, Honiton purlings (braids with a picot edge), Marie

HANDMADE FLEMISH LACE TAPE AND FILLING STITCHES, 1860-1880

Antoinette braids for curtains and bedspreads, Russian braids, point lace braids, and Flemish braids. Black silk braids and purlings were used for decorating the elegant black silk gowns that were an important part of every woman's wardrobe. Even metallic braids were utilized in the making of modern lace. Late in the 19th century, Battenberg braids, as

well as buttons and rings for Royal Battenberg lace, were also

supplied by dry goods stores such as Bloomingdale's as well as lace merchants.

The fragile Bruges braids were most often used for parts of clothing such as collars, cuffs, and insertions. Sometimes Bruges braids were combined with lace motifs and Flemish braids to produce delicate baby bonnets and handkerchiefs.

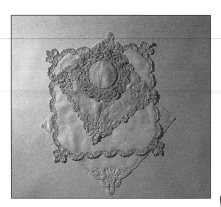

Victorian ladies made handkerchiefs as well as collars, baby bonnets, doilies, and other small furniture coverings from Honiton braids. Larger house-

hold and baby linens were embellished with Ideal Honiton.

Another early form of modern point lace worked by Victorian ladies was called Renaissance braid work. Utilizing an open work braid laid out in geometric patterns drawn or stamped on pink cotton calico, Renaissance braid work was characterized by a single stitch filling each space. The braid was basted to the fabric face side down along the lines of the pattern design.

Then, working from the back side, edges of braid that touched were tacked together with an overcast stitch without catching the fabric. Twisted bars, button-hole bars ornamented with picots, and wheels were used for the filling stitches.

By the early 1890s, tape laces had reached their peak in popularity. The beautiful braid work was prized everywhere. Responding to the demand, new projects and designs for modern lace appeared frequently in the periodicals and journals of the day. Special sections featuring new designs were eagerly awaited by the ladies, and patterns for modern lace stamped on paper or pink calico could be ordered by mail from many of the periodicals and lace merchants. The pink calico was also available with the tape or braid already basted to the fabric — ready for the amateur needlewomen to fill in the needle-point stitches.

The Delineator – "A Journal of Fashion, Culture and Fine Arts" – was published monthly in both London and New York by Butterick Publishing Co., Ltd. Many of the new designs and

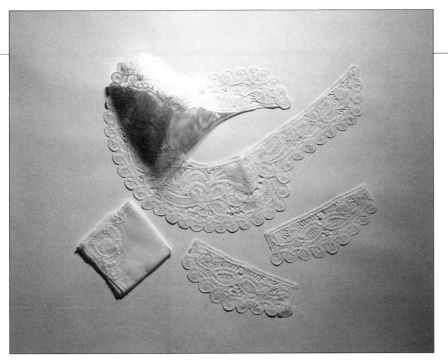

instructions in the modern lace making section of *The Delineator* were contributed by Sarah Hadley. A professional lace maker, Sarah Hadley owned a New York City lace shop in 1894, located at 923 Broadway. Along with supplying various tapes and braids for many styles of modern lace, she designed and supplied many patterns for tape lace projects that delighted Victorian women. Sarah was a master lace crafter, who created many projects in modern lace and Renaissance braid work, with its flat braids and filling stitches, before her work evolved into the heavier Battenberg lace.

The people of the 19th century were called Victorians in honor of the diminutive English queen, whose influence and power spread throughout the British Empire and thus the whole world. Queen Victoria and her consort Prince Albert (the German) had nine children. Their youngest daughter, Princess Beatrice, married another German prince, Henry of Battenberg, in August of 1885. The wedding drew worldwide attention and may have inspired Sarah Hadley

to name her tape lace creation Royal Battenberg.

Characterized by the inclusion of rings and buttons within the filling stitches, Royal Battenberg lace has a sculptural quality that earlier tape laces do not. The distinctive ecru, cream, and white pure linen braids had a vertical/horizontal weave with openwork borders that facilitated the making of precise filling stitches. Instead of guessing the distance between stitches, the lace maker could simply count the openings of the edge. Battenberg and other tape lace making remained a popular hobby until World War I.

A 20th century version of Battenberg lace is still produced commercially in Belgium, where collars and cuffs are often purchased by visitors as a remembrance of the fabulous lace center. China is also a large supplier of the popular Battenberg lace collars, cuffs, and individual motifs, as well as tablecloths and other household linens. Renaissance lace is also still mass produced with a solid tape that is narrower than most of the tapes used for Battenberg lace. The term "Renaissance lace" is used occasionally to designate the 19th century modern tape laces.

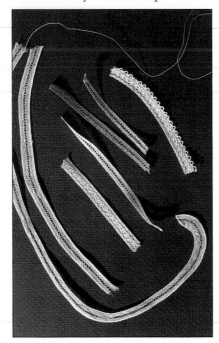

Battenberg lace has become the most commonly used general term for many of the tape laces produced in the 19th century, and it remains popular today. This fun and easy-to-make lace craft was revived during the late 1970s, with lighter, less expensive cotton tapes. By the 1980s, as patterns for the lighter and more delicate new version of the Victorian lace appeared in needlework and sewing magazines, lace makers again enjoyed a pleasant passion for making Battenberg lace.

BASIC INSTRUCTIONS

TAPES AND BRAIDS

Linen braids, which are expensive, have all but disappeared from the catalogs of modern lace merchants. There are, however, many styles of comparably inexpensive cotton tapes or braids available for making Battenberg lace. The most frequently used style is similar to that used in Belgium and has a diagonal weave design with open spaces in the center. It comes in several widths, with 5 mm, 8 mm, and 10 mm being the easiest to work with. The complexity of the pattern and size of the finished project should determine which tape(s) to use. Thus the butterfly and Christmas ornaments in this section were designed with narrow tape (5 mm or 8 mm wide), while the heart pillow and baby bonnet were made with tape that is 10 mm wide. Most tapes or braids are available in white, ecru, and black, as well as gold and silver metallics.

Battenberg lace designs may be traced onto kraft paper or the traditional pink calico; however, a transparent, dissolving (water soluble) stabilizer is a new product that makes Battenberg lace making easier and quicker than ever. The instructions in this section call for the water soluble stabilizer.

A piece of the stabilizer larger than the pattern design is first taped on top of a pattern. Then the design is traced onto the stabilizer with a blue water soluble pen. Removed from the pattern, the stabilizer, inked side underneath, is placed in an embroidery hoop that is about an inch (2-1/2 cm) larger in diameter than the design. The hoop holds the work taut and makes the process much easier.

Tapes or braids have a heavy thread at one edge of the tape. By grasping this thread and pulling with a steady, even motion, the tape will gather evenly to form the various loops and scrolls of the design. When the thread on the other side is pulled, the tape gathers unevenly and the result is very unattractive. If you have difficulty locating the heavy thread, unravel a little at the end of the tape.

The length of tape called for in the instructions varies according to the individual patterns. However, beginners often find that 1-yard (.9 m) tape lengths are a good size for making practice loops. First, mark the center of the tape with a pin, then pull the heavy thread to gather the tape from both ends. The gathers or ease will always form on the inside curve. Keeping this in mind, the three basic design movements—loops, lapped scallops, and reversing the Battenberg tape—are easily formed.

Loops

Loops are the easiest movement because gathered tape seems to have a natural inclination to form them.

1. Starting at point #1, pin the center point of the tape to the stabilizer at the top of a daisy loop.

2. Pull the heavy thread to ease around the fullness of the loop.

3. Follow the arrows of the design crossing the tape at the base of the loop.

4. Continue until all six petals have been formed. Tuck the ends of the tape under the design and pin. Leave a little

extra tape to be cut and glued in place later, and cut the ends. A drop of clear glue will keep the ends of the tape from unraveling. Set aside the daisy you have made for completion with filling stitches later.

When all of the tape has been pinned to the outline daisy design on the stabilizer in the hoop, the next step is to secure the overlapping parts of the tape with a hand sewing needle and #60 fine thread to match the color of the tape or braid. The stitches should be small and blend in with the edge of the tape and the threads where the tape crosses. Secure the gathered inside edges of the loops by overcasting and sewing through the stabilizer. This is the most time-consuming part of the project. Securing the design may also be done with a sewing machine and a narrow zigzag stitch set to catch each side of the tape. This will save a great deal of time; however, the stitches should still blend in with the tape or braid. Machine stitches may not be acceptable if the tape is very fine.

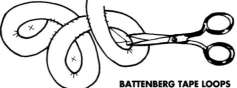

BATTENBERG TAPE LOOPS

Carefully cut away the stabilizer from the spaces formed by the tape's design, leaving the lace attached to the stabilizer, which should be stretched taut in the hoop. A seam ripper is handy for this step, or you may use a pair of embroidery scissors.

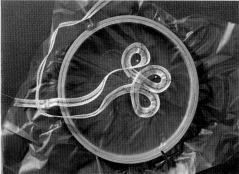

Reversing

Reversing the braid involves bending it back onto itself. This method is often used to form leaves and scrolls. The Fleur-de-lis motif scarf and the tulip heart pillow projects included in this section utilize reversing the braid or tape. With a little of the tape you have left from the daisy, try practicing with the design outline below.

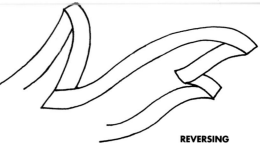

REVERSING

Lapping the braid or tape is used to follow the outline when you do not want to cross one tape over another or to make a scalloped edge effect. The border of the baby bonnet design in this section utilizes the lapped braid technique. A half loop is formed with the tape, and is folded back on itself at the end point. Then the next half loop is formed. Continue until the entire distance of the edging is in place. Try following the outline for a practice edge.

LAPPING

Needlepoint Stitches for Filling the Spaces

The spaces between the tape are filled in with needlepoint stitches. There are many varieties of stitches, but only those used in this chapter's projects are illustrated here. A tapestry needle with a large eye and a point blunt enough to separate and go in between the tapes' woven threads is desirable for the filling stitches. (Regular embroidery needles may penetrate the threads and slow down the stitching, so they're not recommended.)

Cotton crochet or tatting thread is used when using cotton tapes or braids. Linen thread can be used with linen tapes, but it is more expensive. (Even in the

1890s, cotton thread was often substituted for linen.) The finer the thread, the more delicate the stitches. The daisy below was worked with a regular crochet cotton, while the tulip was worked with a heavier thread. Tatting thread would give an even finer result. Since there are times when you will want the stitches to be large and sculptural, and other times when they will be prettier if very delicate, you should experiment before deciding which thread to use.

Needlepoint stitches are generally worked with the single thread strand secured on the wrong side of the lace while it's still in the hoop. The needle is then inserted from the top or right side of the work for each stitch. Tautly stretched spaces produce a more even stitch than loose ones. This is especially important for making rosettes. For edgings or freestanding sculptural projects, the lace may be removed from the hoop.

Point de Bruxelles (Brussels Point)

Point de Bruxelles or Brussels point is the easiest of all the fill-in stitches. Sometimes called the single net stitch, it can be worked in rows from one side of the space to the other or around the edge of an area toward the center or a corner point. This stitch is frequently used to fill in a background area on the projects in this section. The Point de Bruxelles is basically just a buttonhole stitch worked loosely and evenly across the area. Insert the needle from the right side of the work, then on top of the thread, and pull taut to the desired size of the stitch.

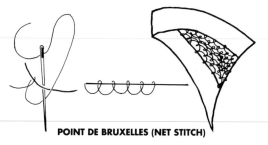

POINT DE BRUXELLES (NET STITCH)

Point de Fillet (Net Groundwork)

Point de fillet or net groundwork stitch is another basic stitch used for filling background spaces. The stitch is worked back and forth in rows and is similar to the Point de Bruxelles stitch, except a knot is made where each stitch loops through another. Secure the thread in a corner of the space to be filled

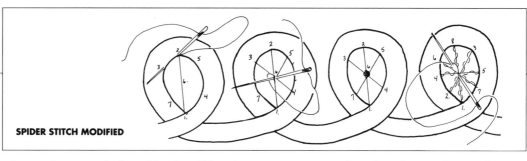

SPIDER STITCH MODIFIED

with a loose buttonhole stitch. Make the knot with a buttonhole stitch by passing the needle under the stitch, then over and under the thread.

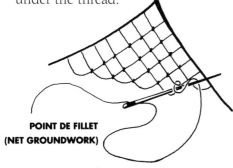

POINT DE FILLET (NET GROUNDWORK)

Russian Stitch

Russian stitch is similar to a herringbone, faggoting, or feather stitch. Extremely versatile, the Russian stitch is used to fill design spaces like leaves and petals, as well as a connecting stitch to attach sections of a project together. After the thread is secured, the needle is inserted from the front of the work on one side, then crosses the thread to the opposite side of the space to a diagonal point situated between the stitches of the first side.

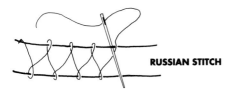

RUSSIAN STITCH

Modified Spider Stitch

Modified spider stitch is an easy, modern version of the more difficult spider stitch detailed below. Used to fill in loops or petals of a daisy, it also works very well to fill triangular-shaped background spaces.

1. Secure the thread at the lowest point of the loop, #1, where the tape crosses. Insert the needle through the tape from the back and take one small stitch in place.

2. Pass the thread across the space to the top of the loop, inserting the needle from the front at point #2. Take an extra stitch in place.

3. Take two small stitches along the edge of the braid to point #3, insert the needle, and take the extra stitch to secure.

4. Pass the thread across the space, inserting the needle at point #4. Take the extra stitch to secure at point #4, then take several small stitches along the braid edge to reach point #5. Secure with an extra stitch. By this time two threads have been extended across the space, crossing at the center or point #6.

5. From point #5, cross the space to the center and make one stitch to connect the threads. Then make one buttonhole stitch on each spoke of the wheel, working from right to left. This will form a knot in the center of the wheel or spider web.

6. The thread is then carried to point #7, where it is secured as before. The final step is to stitch along the edge of the braid and secure at point #1, where you began. The thread may be carried at the back of the lace to the next loop.
   Note: Sometimes eight spokes are used instead of six, with the additional spokes being worked the same as the first six. See illustration for spacing.

Sorrento Wheels (Spiders)

Sorrento wheels or spiders are similar to modified spiders, except there are twisted bars and rosettes in the center instead of a knot. They are used to embellish a focal point of the design because they attract the eye and look very complex. Actually, though, they are really not difficult when practiced a few times and worked step by step.

1. Secure the thread at the lowest point of the loop, #1, where the tape crosses. Stitch along the tape to point #2. Insert the needle through the tape from the back and take one small stitch in place.

137

2. Pass the thread across the space to the top of the loop, inserting the needle from the front at point #3. Take an extra stitch in place. Wrap or twist the thread around the bar several times. (The number of times depends on the width of the bar.)

3. Take two small stitches along the edge of the braid to point #4. Insert the needle and take an extra stitch to secure.

4. Pass the thread across the space, inserting the needle at point #5. Take an extra stitch to secure at point #5, then wrap the thread along the bar, returning to point #4. Take a stitch to secure point #4, then

space to the center and make one stitch to connect the threads. From the center, cross the space to point #1 and take an extra stitch, then twist the bar to the center.

6. Make one buttonhole stitch to secure the bars at the center. Pass the thread over one bar and under the next, continuing around the center for at least three rows but not more than six. Each row should follow the same path as the previous row, which allows every other bar to be raised on top of the rosette formed in the center of the wheel or spider.

7. Carry the thread to point #8, secure, and cut.

The spaces within the loops of the daisy practice motif may be filled with stitches. Work a different stitch in each of the six loops for a sampler, or fill them all with the modified spider stitch. Practicing the needlepoint stitches should prepare you for undertaking the projects included in this section.

PRESSING
Remove the completed Battenberg lace from the stabilizer, and tear away any remaining pieces. Place the completed Battenberg lace face right side down on a clean, padded surface. A piece of muslin laid on top of quilt batting and kept just for this purpose works well.

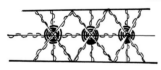

SORRENTO WHEELS

take several small stitches along the braid edge to reach point #6. Secure with an extra stitch. Repeat step 4 for a twisted bar extending from points #6 and #7. By this time three twisted bars have been extended across the space crossing at the center or point #9. Stitch along the edge to point #8 and take a stitch to secure.

5. From point #8, cross the

Note: Sometimes ten (five twisted bars) spokes are used instead of eight (four bars). Another alternative is to work several rosettes along a row of twisted bars. Each rosette must have at least three twisted bars stitched together at a center point by the fourth twisted bar, which intersects each set and forms a rosette at the center point. See illustration for spacing.

Spray sizing on the wrong side of the lace, then cover it with a piece of waxed paper to protect the iron from any remaining pieces of stabilizer. Pre-heat the iron to a medium-heat setting. Place a pressing cloth on top of the waxed paper and press with slow, even strokes. Carefully remove the pressing cloth and the waxed paper while the lace is still warm, and allow the lace to cool before handling.

FLEUR-DE-LIS SCARF

The Fleur-de-lis was the symbol of early France, and it adorned the crown of the Empress Theodora in 527 A.D. In 1179, Charles V selected it for the royal emblem of France, where several fleur-de-lis appeared on the blue field of the coat of arms. The scattered motifs were reduced to three in 1364. England also utilized the "lilies of France" from 1340 to 1801, and the province of Quebec, Canada, still bears the ancient symbol on her flag, with white Fleur-de-lis motifs on a royal blue background.

Fleur-de-lis translates literally to "flower of the lily," and it may have been inspired by the graceful petals of the white Florentine iris. This Fleur-de-lis scarf in Battenberg lace contrasts well with a dark, dressy suit. The scarf can also be arranged on a table with a bouquet of iris or lilies to create a lovely centerpiece. Refer to the basic instructions to review the step-by-step instructions for manipulating the tape and making the filling stitches. Making a few practice pieces before you start the project will increase the quality of your finished piece.

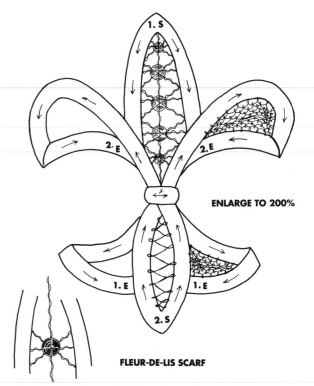

ENLARGE TO 200%

FLEUR-DE-LIS SCARF

**DETAIL OF SORRENTO WHEELS
(TWISTED BARS
WITH ROSETTES)**

**REPEAT FILLING STITCHES
ON LEFT SIDE
S = START
E = END**

MATERIALS NEEDED

4 yards (3.6 m) Battenberg tape

1/6 yard (.15 m) fabric
(Fine linen, batiste, and silk make good choices.)

2 pieces of water-dissolving stabilizer cut into 12-inch (30 cm) squares

10-inch (25 cm) embroidery hoop

Washable marking pen

1 ball white cotton crochet or tatting thread

Tapestry needle

Hand sewing needle and white thread

Fabric or clear glue

Procedure

1. Place one square of washable stabilizer in the hoop. Tighten the hoop for firm, smooth working surface. Trace the Fleur-de-lis pattern on the inside of the stabilizer surface with the pen. Cut the tape into two 1-yard pieces and mark their center points with a pin.

2. Pull the heavy thread at the edge of one tape to gather and shape the tape along the pattern's design. Starting at top of motif, point #1, pin the center of the tape to the stabilizer and shape the point of the upper center loop. Follow the arrows of the diagram down the sides to the lower petals. Start the center of the second piece of tape at the bottom center point #2. Follow the arrows upward to form the upper petals of the design. Cut the tape and tack the ends under the design.

3. Stitch the overlapping parts of the tape with a needle and sewing thread, using tiny stitches along the tape's edges. Secure the gathered edges of the loops by overcasting and sewing through the stabilizer. The stitches should blend in with the tape's threads.

4. Carefully cut the stabilizer away from the spaces formed by the tape's design, leaving the lace attached to the stabilizer in the hoop. Fill in the spaces of the design with decorative stitches using a tapestry needle and crochet or tatting thread. (See illustration, pattern and Basic Instructions.)

5. When all of the fill-in stitches are complete, remove the lace from the hoop and tear away the stabilizer. Place the lace right side down on a pressing surface. Spray sizing on the lace's wrong side, then cover with a piece of waxed paper to prevent bits of stabilizer from sticking to the pressing cloth. Place the pressing cloth on top of the waxed paper and press slowly with an iron that's been pre-heated to a medium-range setting. Waxed paper may stick to the lace, so remove it carefully while the lace is still warm. Allow the lace to cool and then seal the cut edges of the tape with fabric or clear glue on the wrong side of the lace.

6. Hem the long sides of a fabric scarf with a hand-rolled hem. (See page 24.) Pin one of the lace motifs on each end of the scarf with right sides facing up. See diagram. Stitch along the top edge of the motif with tiny overcast stitches, taking care to blend them in with the tape.

7. Working on the wrong side of the scarf, carefully trim away the excess fabric 1/4 inch below line of stitches from Step #4. Turn the fabric edge under and tack with invisible stitches. Press face down on a padded ironing surface.

TULIP HEART PILLOW

Hearts and flowers were popular motifs in Victorian decor, and the heart shape (symbolizing romance) was especially enjoyed as a pillow. This project adds a gracious accent to a bed or couch, and also makes a lovely bridal shower gift.

Although the intricate design of the tulips looks complicated, they are really very easy to make. Refer to the basic instructions to review the step-by-step instructions for manipulating the tape or braid and making the filling stitches.

MATERIALS NEEDED

8-1/2 yards (7.7 m) 10-mm-wide Battenberg tape

1/3 yard (.3 m) fabric (cotton, linen, or silk)

CONTINUED ON PAGE 144

DOILY SLEEP PILLOW

This sleep pillow was made by gluing a Battenberg lace doily to a heart pillow and filling it with
fragrant herbs or potpourri. The pillow adds a
Victorian accent to bedrooms and sitting rooms,
and allows you to enjoy the fragrance of your
favorite garden blooms year 'round.

CONTINUED ON PAGE 146

$\mathcal{T}$ULIP HEART PILLOW

MATERIALS NEEDED (cont.)

1/3 yard cotton batting or fiber filling for stuffing

20-inch (50 cm) square piece of water-dissolving stabilizer

12-inch (30 cm) embroidery hoop

Washable marking pen

1 ball white cotton crochet or tatting thread

Tapestry needle

Sewing machine and #60 white thread

Fabric glue

PROCEDURE

1. Place the stabilizer in the hoop, and tighten for a firm, smooth working surface. Trace the tulip heart pattern onto the inside of the stabilizer surface with a washable marking pen.

2. Mark the center point of a 2-yard (1.8 m) piece of Battenberg tape with a pin. Working on the top side of the hoop, pin the tape to the stabilizer at the center loop at the bottom of the heart.

3. Pull the heavy thread at the edge of one tape to gather and shape it along pattern design. Starting at center point #1 (see diagram), shape the loop at the base of the heart. Follow the arrows of the diagram along the tulip stems. Cut the tape, leaving a short length to be covered by the tulip tape.

Starting at point #2, form the first tulip. Repeat for second tulip, starting at point #3. Then form the two side loops at the bottom of the heart and the two lower leaves. The cut ends of tape should be concealed under the loop of the design.

4. Cut a second 2-yard piece of tape for the center leaf and the heart's top loops. Follow the instructions above and the numbers for starting each new piece of tape. Set the remaining tape aside until you've completed Steps 5 and 6.

5. Machine zigzag the overlapping parts of the tape along the edges with #60 thread and narrow stitches. Secure adjoining tape edges to each other and trim the threads. The stitches should blend in with tape's threads. Carefully cut away the stabilizer from the spaces formed by the tape's design, leaving the lace attached to the stabilizer in the hoop.

6. Fill in the spaces of the design with decorative stitches using tapestry needle and crochet or tatting thread. The rosette bars in the tulip's centers are made with single bars except for the center bar, which is twisted. Use the basic instructions and the pattern for guidance.

7. Mark the center point of the remaining length of tape and form a loop about 2 inches (5 cm) deep at the bottom of the heart. Form loops around the edge of the heart about 1-1/2 inches (4 cm) high and 1-5/8 inches (4-1/2 cm) wide

where they touch at each side. The loops may vary a little as they surround the heart and the basic form changes, but they should meet at the top. Remove the hoop.

8. Machine zigzag stitch the loops to the heart and where the tapes cross at each loop. Work a rosette stitch on double-twisted bars in the center space at the top, and a modified spider stitch in each loop. When all fill-in stitches are complete, tear away stabilizer.

9. Place the lace right side down on a padded surface. Spray sizing on the lace's wrong side, then cover with a piece of wax paper to prevent bits of stabilizer from sticking to the pressing cloth. Place the pressing cloth on top of the waxed paper and press

slowly with an iron that's been pre-heated to a medium-range setting. The waxed paper may stick to lace, so remove it while the lace is still warm. Allow the lace to cool and then seal the cut edges of the tape with clear glue on the wrong side of the lace.

10. Cut two hearts from fabric for the pillow. With right sides together, stitch the heart, leaving about 3 inches (7 cm) on one side for stuffing. Turn the pillow right side out and insert stuffing. Insert additional pieces into the pillow's center until it's thick. Close the opening with a blind stitch.

11. Pin the lace motif on the right side of the fabric pillow. Stitch along the motif's edges with tiny overcast stitches, taking care to blend them in with the tape.

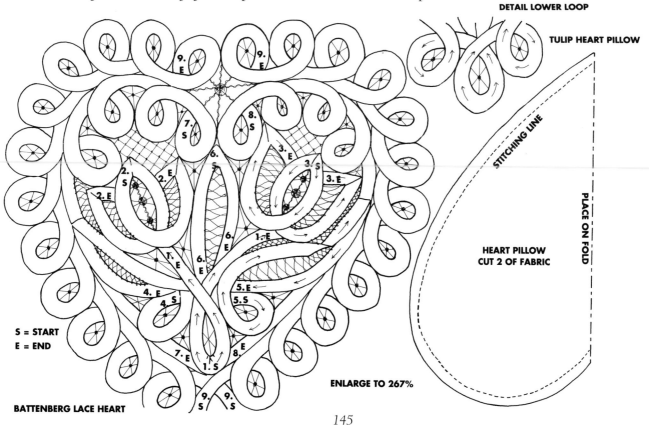

DETAIL LOWER LOOP

TULIP HEART PILLOW

STITCHING LINE

PLACE ON FOLD

HEART PILLOW
CUT 2 OF FABRIC

S = START
E = END

ENLARGE TO 267%

BATTENBERG LACE HEART

145

DOILY SLEEP PILLOW

MATERIALS NEEDED

Battenberg lace doily, 6 inches (15 cm) in diameter

1/2 yard (.5 m) silk, peau-de-soie, satin, taffeta, or linen

1/2 yard fine net or illusion veiling, 60 inches (1.5 m) wide

1 yard Battenberg or other narrow braid

Hand sewing needle and thread

Fabric glue

Dried, fragrant herbs (*Note:* The oils in commercially prepared potpourris may stain the lace.)

PROCEDURE

1. Trace the heart pattern onto tissue paper and cut out three hearts from the fine net or veiling. With net attached to the pattern, place it on the fabric for the pillow back and cut one. From the remaining fabric, cut a 5- x 60-inch (.1 x 1.5 m) strip for a ruffle around the edge of the heart. *Note:* The ruffle may be made of the net or the backing fabric.

2. Place the Battenberg doily in the center of one piece of the net or illusion veiling. Secure it in place with fabric glue dotted sparingly on the back of the doily. Set aside to dry. If you prefer, you can baste the doily in place and then whipstitch or overcast it to the net, following the inside edge of the tape pattern. The tiny hand stitches should be almost invisible. Machine straight stitch about 1/4 inch (6 mm) from the edge of the remaining two pieces of net of each size, leaving about 3 inches (7 cm) open along one edge. Trim seam. Turn right side out to make a bag and fill with fragrant herbs or rose petals. Close the opening with tiny hand overcast stitches.

3. Fold the ruffle strip in half lengthwise and stitch two gathering rows on the sewing machine. Pull threads to gather.

4. Pin the ruffle around the edge of pillow back, allowing 1/4 inch for the seam. (The finished edge of the ruffle should face the middle of the pillow back.) Start pinning at the top center of the heart, and tack the ruffle ends at the center. Baste, then machine stitch.

5. Place the net and back with ruffle right sides together. The finished ruffle and the doily lace will be inside. Baste about 1/4 inch from the edge, leaving a 3-inch opening on one side. Turn right side out.

6. Insert the herb-filled net bags into the pillows directly behind the top lace appliquéd net. Overcast stitch the opening with tiny stitches to close.

7. Stitch or glue the Battenberg or other narrow braid to the edge of the heart to cover the seam, starting at the center top. Tuck the ends of the ruffle under the braid. Conceal the ends of the braid under the top point of the doily.

ℬATTENBERG ℬABY ℬONNET ❀ ❀ ❀

*T*his Battenberg baby bonnet was inspired by a point lace infant's cap design from the August 1857 issue of *Godey's Lady's Book*. Popular during the mid-1850s, this type of lace (known as "point" or "tape" lace) was made from tapes and braids that were machine-made or homemade on a pillow as bobbin lace. Filling stitches were then added with the same stitches used for handmade needlepoint lace.

Although the bonnet is an advanced skill level project, it looks more difficult than it really is. The crown and two sides of the bonnet are worked as separate pieces and then assembled after completion. The scalloped edge is added after the other pieces are stitched together. Refer to the basic instructions to review the step-by-step instructions for manipulating the tape or braid and making the filling stitches.

MATERIALS NEEDED
- 8 yards (7.2 m) Battenberg tape
- 14-inch (36 cm) square piece of water-dissolving stabilizer
- 2 strips stabilizer, each measuring 9 x 1 inches (22 x 2-1/2 cm)
- 12-inch (30 cm) embroidery hoop
- Washable marking pen
- Silver marking pencil
- 1 yard (.9 m) double-sided white ribbon, 5/8 inch (15 mm) wide
- 1 ball white cotton crochet or tatting thread
- Tapestry needle
- Regular hand sewing needle and white thread
- Fabric or clear glue

147

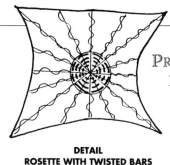

DETAIL
ROSETTE WITH TWISTED BARS

PROCEDURE

1. Place the square of stabilizer in the hoop, and tighten the hoop for a firm, smooth working surface. Trace the bonnet pattern onto the inside of the stabilizer surface with a washable marking pen.

2. Mark the center point of a 2-yard (1.8 m) length of tape with a pin. Working on the top side of the hoop, pin the tape to the stabilizer at the center front of the crown section's intertwining loop. Pull the heavy thread at the edge of one tape to gather and shape the tape along the pattern's design. Starting at center point #1, shape the center loop of the crown motif. Follow the arrows of the diagram along the crown to the end loops and back. Hide the cut ends of tape by tacking them under the center of the end loop's design.

3. Each daisy side motif will require about 1 yard of tape. Follow the instructions above and the numbers for starting each new piece of tape at the center (point #1). Follow the pattern to outline the crown and side motifs with the tape, pulling the thread to ease the tape and creasing it at the corners.

4. Stitch the overlapping parts of the tape with a needle and sewing thread, using tiny stitches along the tape's edges. Secure the gathered edges of the loops by overcasting and sewing through the stabilizer. The stitches should blend in with the tape's threads.

5. Carefully cut away the stabilizer from the spaces formed by the tape's design, leaving the lace attached to the stabiliz-er in the hoop. Fill in the spaces of the design with decorative stitches using a tapestry needle and crochet or tatting thread. Fill the centers of the small loops with a modified spider stitch with four bars. Fill the large spaces of the side motifs with the netting stitch, and fill the crown motif's large spaces with double-twisted bars and rosettes. Fill two of the small loops on the crown motif with the Russian stitch. Use the basic instructions, the pattern, and the illustration for guidance.

6. When all of the fill-in stitches are complete, remove the lace from the hoop and tear away the stabilizer. Place the lace right side down on a padded surface. Spray sizing on the lace's wrong side, then cover with a piece of waxed paper to prevent bits of stabilizer from sticking to the pressing cloth. Place the pressing cloth on top of the waxed paper and press slowly with an iron pre-heated to a medium-range setting. The waxed paper may stick to the lace, so remove it while the lace is still warm. Allow the lace to cool and then seal the cut edges of the tape with clear glue on the wrong side of the lace.

7. Pin the strips of stabilizer along both sides of the crown. Then pin the sides to the stabilizer, leaving about 1/4 inch (6 mm) of space between the two pieces of Battenberg lace. Starting at the front of the bonnet and working toward the back, work a Russian stitch, picking up one stitch from the crown and one from the side motif. Repeat for the other side. Remove the stabilizer and press as directed in Step 6.

8. With pins or a silver pencil, mark off 1-inch (2-1/2 cm) intervals all around the bonnet's edge for the scallops. Attach the center of a 2-yard piece of tape at the first point near the center front of the crown motif. Pull the thread and gently form the scallop loops, creasing the tape at each marked point. End the tape at the back of the bonnet, and use fabric or clear glue to keep the ends from raveling. Attach ribbon at the front corners.

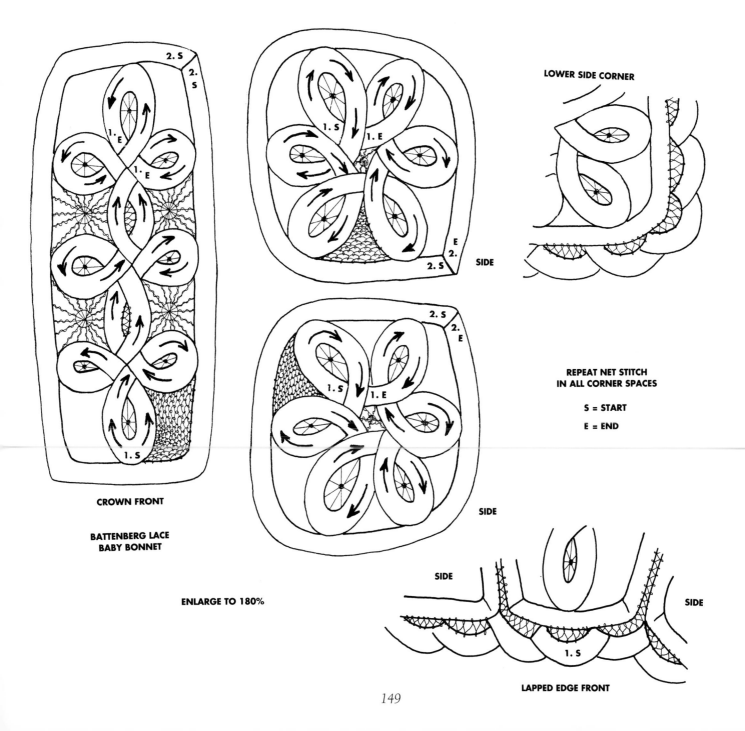

LOWER SIDE CORNER

REPEAT NET STITCH
IN ALL CORNER SPACES

S = START

E = END

CROWN FRONT

BATTENBERG LACE
BABY BONNET

SIDE

SIDE

SIDE

SIDE

ENLARGE TO 180%

LAPPED EDGE FRONT

CONTINUED ON PAGE 152

Butterflies were popular motifs for the Victorians, who loved intricate, delicate designs. Experience with making at least one other Battenberg lace project is recommended before undertaking this butterfly,

although it's not as difficult as it looks. Refer to the basic instructions for step-by-step instructions for manipulating the tape or braid and making the filling stitches.

POTPOURRI BIRDS

𝒯he lace for these three-dimensional birds was created on a flat surface with tape and simple filling stitches. The lace was then attached to a wire armature and a tulle body filled with fragrant potpourri.

The standing bird looks nice displayed on a bookcase shelf or on an end table, while the flying bird looks lovely arranged in a bouquet of flowers or a wreath.

CONTINUED ON PAGE 156

151

Butterfly

Materials Needed

6 yards (5.4 m) narrow Battenberg tape

1/3 yard (.3 m) fabric (linen or silk)

1/3 yard cotton or fiber batting

Frame with 2 pieces of cardboard backing

14-inch (36 cm) square piece of water-dissolving stabilizer

12-inch (30 cm) embroidery hoop

Washable marking pen

1 ball white crochet cotton or tatting thread

Tapestry needle

Regular hand sewing needle and #60 white thread

Fabric or clear glue

Procedure

1. Place the stabilizer in the hoop, and tighten for a firm, smooth working surface. Trace the butterfly pattern onto the inside of the stabilizer surface with a washable marking pen.

2. Mark the center point of a 2-yard (1.8 m) piece of Battenberg tape with pins. Working on the top side of the hoop, pin the tape to the stabilizer just below the head at the center of the upper wings. Pull the heavy thread at edge of one tape to gather and shape the tape along the pattern's design. Starting at center point #1, shape the center point of the upper wings. Follow the arrows of the diagram along the wing to completely delineate the wing, then crease the tape and make the loops inside the wing. Repeat for the other upper wing. Cut the tape a little beyond point #2. Tack the cut ends of the tape under the loop of the design.

3. Each of the lower wings requires about 1 yard (.9 m) of tape. Follow the instructions above and the numbers for starting and ending a new piece of tape. Fold and pin the feelers at the center. Use the small, leftover pieces of tape for the body, head, and feelers.

4. Stitch the overlapping parts of the tape with a needle and sewing thread, using tiny stitches along the tape's edges. Secure the gathered edges of the loops by overcasting and sewing through the stabilizer. The stitches should blend in with the tape's threads.

5. Carefully cut away the stabilizer from the spaces formed by the tape's design, leaving the lace attached to the stabilizer in the hoop. Fill in the spaces of the design with decorative stitches using a tapestry needle and crochet or tatting thread. Use the basic instructions and the pattern for guidance.

6. When all of the fill-in stitches are complete, remove the lace from the hoop and tear away the stabilizer. Place the lace right side down on a padded surface. Spray sizing on the lace's wrong side, then cover with a piece of waxed paper to prevent bits of stabilizer from sticking to the pressing cloth. Place the pressing cloth on top of the waxed paper and press slowly with an iron that's been pre-heated to a medium-range setting. The waxed paper may

stick to lace, so remove it while the lace is still warm. Allow the lace to cool and then seal the cut edges of the tape with clear glue on the wrong side of the lace.

7. Cut a piece of batting the same size as the frame's cardboard backing, and then cut a piece of fabric 1 inch (2-1/2 cm) larger than the cardboard backing. Place the fabric-covered batting over the cardboard backing.

8. Pin the butterfly motif on the right side of the fabric. Stitch along the edge of the center of the motif with tiny overcast stitches, taking care to blend them in with the tape. Turn over and glue or tape the edge of the fabric to the back of the cardboard. Cover the back with the second piece of cardboard and frame.

ENLARGE TO 155%

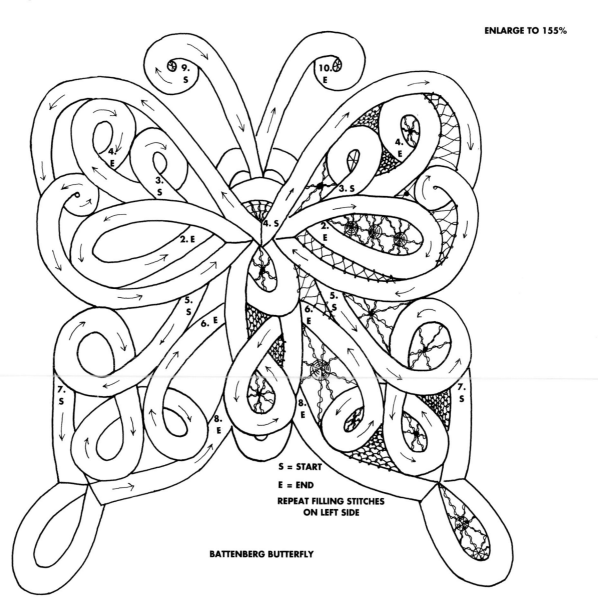

S = START
E = END
REPEAT FILLING STITCHES
ON LEFT SIDE

BATTENBERG BUTTERFLY

153

CHRISTMAS TREE SKIRT

This beautiful tree skirt makes the holidays even more festive and lends its special loveliness to the gifts displayed around it. If you don't tell, no one will know that the doilies are ready-made, and that you didn't spend many hours making the Battenberg circle motifs by hand.

MATERIALS NEEDED

5 Battenberg lace doilies, 7-1/2 inches (18 cm) in diameter

1 Battenberg lace doily, 6 inches (15 cm) in diameter

5 Battenberg lace doilies, 4-1/2 inches (11 cm) in diameter

18- x 18-inch (46 cm) square of fabric (linen, cotton, or a blend)

Spray sizing

Washable marking pen (color should contrast with fabric)

Sharp scissors

Spool of thread to match doilies

Spool of thread to match fabric

Ball white cotton crochet or tatting
thread

Regular hand sewing needle and white
thread

Sheet of cardboard

Fabric glue

Snap fastener or 1 yard (.9 m) ribbon

PROCEDURE

1. Wash and press the fabric; press the
   doilies with a steam iron and spray
   sizing. Mark an 18-inch circle on
   the square of fabric and place it on
   the cardboard for a smooth, firm
   working surface.

2. Mark the center point of the circle
   and draw two lines radiating from
   this point to the edge of the fabric,
   where they will be 1 inch (2-1/2
   cm) apart. (See illustration.)

3. Cut away the center of a medium-
   sized doily and place it on the center of the fabric. Draw around the
   opening to make a hole for the tree
   trunk. Carefully cut an opening in
   the doily by removing the design
   threads to separate the edges.

4. Seal the cut edges on the back side
   of the doily with clear glue. With a
   sewing machine and thread to match
   the fabric, straight stitch along the
   lines from the edge to the center,
   then around the center opening,
   and then back to the edge.

5. Set the machine on a narrow zigzag
   and sew over the first stitching lines.

Carefully trim the fabric away close
to the stitching line and press.

6. Set the machine on a slightly wider
   zigzag stitch and sew over the first
   line of zigzag stitches. Press the
   edges of the opening to the back
   for a neat finish.

7. Place the center of a medium-sized
   doily on the right side of the fabric
   with the pattern design lined up
   with the openings. Baste in place.
   Arrange the large doilies on the
   edge of the fabric in a star point
   position with the right sides facing
   up. Place a small doily between
   each large doily with the edges
   touching. (See illustration.) Baste.

8. Change the top thread in the sewing
   machine to match the doilies. Set the
   machine to a narrow zigzag and stitch
   along the edge of the center doily and
   the top edges of the large and small
   doilies. (Or, the doilies may be glued
   in place with fabric glue.)

9. Turn the skirt over to the back side
   and carefully trim away the excess
   fabric 1/4 inch (6 mm) from the line
   of stitches away from the large and
   small doilies. Turn the fabric edge
   under at the back opening and tack
   with invisible stitches or glue.

10. Connect the doilies where they
    touch with crochet cotton and a
    tapestry needle. Press the skirt face
    down on a well-padded surface.
    Add the snap fastener or ribbon
    to close at the center back.

Note: For a larger tree skirt, purchase
larger doilies and use a 20-inch (50 cm)
square of fabric.

PATTERN
TULLE
BODY

DIAGRAM FOR TAPE
AND STITCHES
S = START
E = END

ENLARGE TO 230%

ℙOTPOURRI BIRDS

𝒯he lace for these three-dimensional birds was created on a flat surface with tape and simple filling stitches. The lace was then attached to a wire armature and a tulle body filled with fragrant potpourri. The standing bird looks nice displayed on a bookcase shelf or on an end table, while the flying bird looks lovely arranged in a bouquet of flowers or a wreath.

MATERIALS NEEDED

2 yards (1.8 m) Battenberg tape

1/8 yard (.1 m) white tulle

12-inch (30 cm) square of water-dissolving stabilizer

10-inch (25 cm) embroidery hoop

Washable marking pen

Ball white cotton crochet or tatting thread

2 pieces of medium-gauge floral wire, one measuring 18 inches (46 cm) and one measuring 8 inches (20 cm)

Tapestry needle

Hand sewing needle and white thread

Fabric or clear glue

White floral tape or narrow ribbon

Dried fragrant herbs and colorful flowers (Larkspur and annual statice were used for the standing birds, while rose petals were used for the flying birds.)

PROCEDURE

1. Form the body by bending the 18-inch length of wire into a loop with an open end. (See illustration.) Twist the wire to form the head and body sections, leaving about 2 inches (5 cm) of wire at each end for the legs. Squeeze the wire to a point for the beak. (The beak should be on the side of the head for the standing bird or the top of the head for the flying bird.) Fold the 8-inch length of wire in half and loop it around the lower body, twisting to secure. Next, fold the ends back to form the feet. (For the standing bird, the wire feet are manipulated until it balances; for the flying bird, the legs and feet should be straight back.)

2. To form the body cover, cut out a double thickness of tulle from the pattern. Check to make sure the tulle is at least 1/4 inch (6 mm) wider than the armature for the seam allowance.

   Stitch by hand or machine through both thicknesses, beginning below the neck on one side and leaving one side open. Trim the seam allowance to 1/8 inch (3 mm) and turn right sides out.

3. Fit the tulle form loosely over the armature. Gradually fill the head with potpourri or cotton stuffing until the head is full and well shaped. Carefully stuff the rest of the bird, stopping frequently to sew the area where you've just stuffed. Be sure to pack the stuffing tight and to securely stitch the tulle, anchoring it to the bottom of the body and the top of the legs.

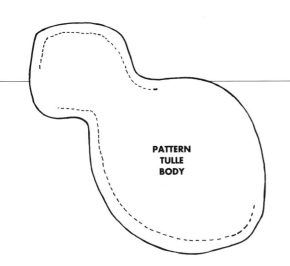

**PATTERN
TULLE
BODY**

**BATTENBERG LACE BIRD
STANDING BIRD (A)**

ENLARGE TO 216%

**DIAGRAM FOR TAPE
AND STITCHES**

S = START

E = END

4. To begin forming the lace, place the stabilizer inside the hoop and tighten it until you have a working surface that's smooth and firm. Trace the lace pattern on the inside of the stabilizer with a washable marking pen. Mark the center point of the tape with a pin.

5. Pull the heavy thread at the edge of the tape to gather and shape it along the pattern's design. Pin the center of the tape to the stabilizer at point #1 and shape the side loops up and back to the head for the standing bird. Cut the tape and tack the cut ends under the design. Add the wings, beak, and crest from the remaining pieces of tape. (The flying bird is one continuous piece of tape for the body and wings. Begin at the head and continue following the pattern; then add the beak at the top of the head.)

6. Stitch the overlapping parts of the tape with needle and sewing thread, using tiny stitches along the tape edges. Secure the gathered edges of loops by overcasting and sewing through the stabilizer. The stitches should blend in with the tape threads. Carefully cut the stabilizer away from the spaces formed by the tape design, leaving the lace attached to the stabilizer and still in the hoop. Fill in the design spaces with decorative stitches using a tapestry needle and crochet or tatting thread. Refer to the illustrations and the pattern as you work.

7. After you've completed the fill-in stitches, remove the lace from the hoop and tear away the stabilizer. Place the lace face down on a padded surface and spray with a light layer of sizing. Cover the lace with a piece of wax paper and press slowly. Remove the wax paper while the lace is still warm to prevent sticking.

8. After the lace has cooled, seal the cut edges of the lace with clear glue or a commercial product designed for this purpose. Pin the lace onto the potpourri-filled bird body, fitting along the rear seam first. Stitch the top of the two head sections together with fine thread, starting at the back below the crest and working until you reach just below the beak.

9. Use a tapestry needle to attach a length of crochet or tatting thread to the left side of the head under the beak. Cross to the right side of the head, leaving an opening for the first net stitch. Turn for the second row, looping the thread through the center of the previous net stitch. Continue to attach the lace to the body with net stitches, increasing and decreasing the number of stitches in each row as needed and

BATTENBERG ORNAMENTS

*I*nspired by some hand blown glass antique Christmas balls that had been decorated with a metallic braid, these Battenberg ornaments make a fun and easy afternoon project. Detailed instructions for the filling stitches are included in the basic information at the beginning of this section.

MATERIALS NEEDED FOR EACH BALL

1-1/2 yards (1.4 m) silver or gold metallic Battenberg tape

Plastic ball ornament that separates in half, 3-1/2 inches (8 cm) in diameter

Marking pen

1 ball metallic crochet or tatting thread

Tapestry needle

Clear glue

Christmas potpourri

PROCEDURE

1. Fill the ball with potpourri and seal with a drop of glue. Cut the tape into four pieces, one measuring 14 inches (36 cm), one measuring 13 inches (33 cm), and two measuring 12 inches (30 cm).

2. Glue the ends of the 14-inch length of tape to the bottom of the ball at the seam. Then glue it along the seam until both pieces meet at the center top. The extra tape at the top will form a loop hanger.

3. Mark the ball into eight equal sections. (See diagram.) Starting at the top of the ball, wrap one 12-inch length of tape around the ball at point #2, and the other length at point #3. Glue the ends and then dot more glue sparingly along the seam.

4. Start the 13-inch length at the top so it covers the ends of the other tapes. The extra inch will form a decorative loop at the bottom of the ornament. Allow the tape to dry for several hours.

5. Fill in the spaces of the design with decorative stitches using a tapestry needle and metallic crochet or tatting thread. The Russian stitch quickly fills seven of the spaces between the tapes. Double twisted bars and rosettes fill the eighth space, or you may fill all spaces with the Russian stitch.

BIBLIOGRAPHY

Altman. *Altman Quarterly*. New York City, New York: B. Altman & Co., 1925

Barnhart, Robert K. *Barnhart Dictionary of Etymology*. United States: The H. W. Wilson Co., 1988.

Baumgartel, Beth. "Manufactured Fibers," *Vogue Patterns* November/December, 1992 and January/February 1993.

Bloomingdale, Brthers Bryk, and Villa, Nancy. *Bloomingdale's 1886 Illustrated Catalog*. New York City, New York: Dover Publications, Inc., 1988/1886.

Blum, Stella. *Fashions and Costumes from Godey's Lady's Book*. New York City, New York: Dover Publications, Inc., 1985.

Britannica. *New Encyclopedia Britannica*, Volumes 4, 7, 28. Chicago, Illinois: Encyclopedia Britannica, 1990.

Bullock, Alice-May. *Lace and Lacemaking*. New York City, New York: Larousse & Co. Inc., 1981.

C.H.A.N. Sein-Jurado, Eunice. *Battenberg Lace: More of its History & Variations*. Tallahassee, Florida: Sein-Jurado-Bas, 1991.

Caulfield, Sophia Saward, Blanche. *Dictionary of Needlework*. Exeter, England: Blaketon Hall, Ltd., 1989/1885.

Cave, Oenone. *Cut-Work Embroidery and How to Do It*. New York City, New York: Dover Publications, Inc., 1982/1963.

Coats, J & P. *Anchor Manual Needlework*. Loveland, Colorado: Interweave Press, 1990/1958.

Coleman, Elizabeth. *Fashions of the Opulent Era, Vintage Fashions*. Cumberland, Maryland: Hobby House Press, Inc., 1990.

Collier's. *Collier's Encyclopedia*, Volumes 6, 10, and 14. New York City, New York: P. F. Collier, Inc., 1989.

Collier, Ann. *The Art of Lacemaking*. London, England: Bracken Books, 1989.

Davenport, Milla. *The Book of Costume*, Volume I. New York City, New York: Crown Publishers, Inc., 1970/1948.

Earnshaw, Pat. *Lace Machines and Machine Laces*. London, England: Batsford, Ltd., 1986.

Fanning, Robbie Singer. *Singer Instructions for Art Embroidery & Lace Work*. Menlo Park, California: Open Chain Publishing Co., 1989/1922.

Frost, Annie S. *Ladies' Guide to Needlework*. Mendocino, California: R. L. Shep, 1877/1986.

Fuhrmann, Brigita. *Bobbin Lace*. New York City, New York:: Dover Publications, Inc., 1985.

Gardner, Helen. *Art through the Ages*. New York City, NY: Harcourt Brace, and World:1970/1926.

Gernsheim, Alison. *Victorian & Edwardian Fashion: A Photographic Survey*. New York City, New York: Dover Publications, Inc., 1981.

Godey, Louis A. and Hale, Sarah J. *Godey's Lady's Book and Magazine*. Philadelphia, Pennsylvania: Louis A. Godey, 1857.

Grolier. *Academic American Encyclopedia*, Volumes K–L. Danbury, Connecticut: Grolier, Inc., 1983.

Hadley, Sara, Ed. *Battenberg and Other Tape Laces*. Mineola, New York: Dover Publications, Inc., 1988/1901.

Harper & Brothers. *Harper's Bazaar*, Volume XXIL -No. 4. New York City, New York: Harper & Brothers, 1889.

CONTINUED ON PAGE 160

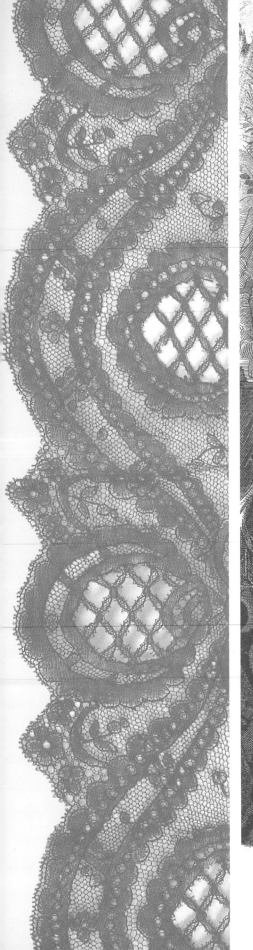

Engraved &

LES MODES PARISIENN

DECEM